THE RULE OF SAINT BENEDICT

ST. BENEDICT OF NURSIA

A CONTEMPORARY PARAPHRASE BY
JONATHAN WILSON-HARTGROVE

PARACLETE PRESS
BREWSTER, MASSACHUSETTS

The Rule of Saint Benedict: A Contemporary Paraphrase – The Paraclete Essentials Deluxe Edition

2015 First Printing This Edition

Copyright © 2012 by Jonathan Wilson-Hartgrove

ISBN 978-1-61261-769-5

The Paraclete Press name and logo (dove on cross) are trademarks of Paraclete Press, Inc.

The Library of Congress has catalogued the original edition of this book as follows:

Wilson-Hartgrove, Jonathan, 1980-
  The Rule of Saint Benedict : a contemporary paraphrase / by Jonathan Wilson-Hartgrove.
     p. cm. — (Paraclete essentials)
  Includes bibliographical references (p.   ).
  ISBN 978-1-55725-973-8 (trade pbk.)
  1. Benedict, Saint, Abbot of Monte Cassino. Regula.—Paraphrases. I. Benedict, Saint, Abbot of Monte Cassino. Regula. II. Title.
  BX3004.E6 2012
  255'.10—dc23   2011051384

10 9 8 7 6 5 4 3 2 1

Published by Paraclete Press
Brewster, Massachusetts
www.paracletepress.com
Printed in China

CONTENTS

INTRODUCTION

The little book that you're holding in your hands is the product of one person's attempt to distill the treasures of a tradition he inherited and to pass on their essential wisdom for life with God and other people. *The Rule of Saint Benedict* was originally written to serve a few communities in sixth-century Italy and might have easily been lost, as hundreds of similar documents no doubt were. But it wasn't lost. Instead, it became a spiritual classic and one of the most important texts in Western civilization.

The story of *The Rule of Saint Benedict* is the story of how a small movement within Christianity changed the landscape of the world for everyone. This movement existed before the *Rule* was written, springing up in the Egyptian deserts during the fourth century. There women and men who longed to know true life in Christ devoted themselves to prayer, intentionally distancing themselves from a society that was in shambles—despite the fact that it was becoming "Christian" in name. Because these men and women devoted themselves to one thing only—to the love of God—these experimenters on the edges of Christendom were called *monastics* (from the Greek *monos*, meaning *one*).

By the end of the fifth century, when a middle-class, young Italian named Benedict left his home in Nursia to go to school in Rome, the Empire that had been centered there was in total disarray. The church whose faith had become the official religion of that Empire was in turmoil. It was in every way a time of transition. In short, it was a moment not unlike our own.

Everyone knew that a new future was being born, but no one was sure just what it would look like.

In a moment of clarity, Benedict saw that the system of education that had been designed to prepare him for a world that was passing away could only lead to a dead end. While it could teach him what had worked in the past, the system did not have the resources to present a way forward. A different kind of school was needed. Benedict had a hunch that the Desert Mothers and Fathers were creating it. He went to a cave, built himself a prayer cell, and so matriculated in the "university" of the world-to-come.

Any student of the desert tradition quickly learns what its first practitioners experienced: an authentic search for God leads to life with other people. The peculiar new society that emerges in this common life needs a structure. So there are rules. A "rule of life" is an attempt to put down on paper the way that a small group of people agree to live together so that their every effort moves them closer to God. When Benedict submitted himself to the wisdom of the desert school, these rules became his textbooks.

So it happened that when others came to ask Benedict for guidance—and when these people ultimately called him to lead their community—he brought with him both the knowledge that can only be gained through practice and the collective wisdom handed down from those who'd gone before him. We know for certain that the latter included John Cassian's *Institutes* and *Conferences*, Basil of Caesarea's *Rule*, a document called *The Rule of the Master* among others. In other words, when the time came to craft his own rule, Benedict did not start from scratch.

He edited—even paraphrased—rules that others had written, modifying them as he saw fit to make them workable; to make them memorable; to make them a curriculum for a new kind of education. This way of learning, Benedict said, would be a "school for the Lord's service."

Of course, Benedict had no way of knowing the historical significance of the work he was writing. Fifteen hundred years later, we can look back and see that this articulation of the desert's wisdom became determinative for Western monasticism. It has guided communities that have produced a disproportionate number of saints and created the seedbeds for democracy and abolition, public education and hospitals. Throughout the Middle Ages, Benedictine communities gave birth to the schools where people learned to imagine a new society within the shell of the old. They were training centers for clergy and scholars; centers for the preservation of ancient manuscripts; havens for the arts; sources for spiritual direction; and houses of hospitality for those in need. These communities became literal schools for the world-to-come. But for Benedict in the sixth century, the *Rule* could only have been an honest attempt to say in the present what a tradition of radical commitment to the gospel offered people who wanted to shape a life together.

So, then, what about the future? At the beginning of the twenty-first century, when almost every sign points to the fact that we are, all of us, in the midst of a great social and cultural transition, many people are experimenting with new forms of life together, trying to imagine what the future will hold for them and for the human community. Our existing educational institutions can serve well to train people in a way of life that has worked for generations. But a growing number of people, young and older, sense that this way of life leads them to a dead end. We need spaces to imagine new possibilities, places to remember that another world is possible. We're thirsty for the good news of a new heaven and a new earth.

We need a school for a new way of life.

Within the Christian tradition, the monastic stream is the source that has consistently offered formational resources for a new way of life in new circumstances. We never start from scratch. Instead, we learn from the practice of prayer and life together as we take from the storehouse "some things old and some things new." There is, indeed, a great storehouse of wisdom in the Christian classics. Like Benedict, we do well to immerse ourselves in them. And, like Benedict, we have to translate that truth for our own day.

This paraphrase of Benedict's classic *Rule* is an attempt to present monastic wisdom as a curriculum for finding our common future together. It grows out of my own practice of prayer and action in the new monastic community called Rutba House in Durham, North Carolina. While Benedict's *Rule* is not our community's rule, we have learned from it, as Benedict learned from Basil and the Master before him. Listening to the *Rule* alongside our life together, I've become convinced that Benedict is a prophet for our time. My experience says, "Listen to him." Even when it feels difficult, I keep listening.

This listening brings me back to the *Rule*, reading not so much for inspiration as for direction. In the early sixth century, when Benedict was still living in a cave outside of Rome, pilgrims began coming to ask him for spiritual guidance—a "word" of wisdom for their own lives. Time and again, I too have come to the *Rule* for a "word" about how to keep living together in a world that's falling apart. As an American evangelical who was raised with the Bible, I immediately recognized in Benedict someone who took Scripture every bit as seriously as the people who raised me. Not only does he believe every word of it to be true, but he clearly thinks every word of it has something to say about how we should live.

The *Rule*, then, is more like a sermon than a self-help book. It does not offer fourteen ways to enrich your prayer life or to improve your relationship with neighbors. Instead, it outlines in very concrete terms what it looks like for a community of people to live their whole life according to the truth of the gospel. In very specific ways, it tells you what to do. It does not suggest. It proclaims.

As a contemporary reader of the *Rule*, I am tempted to "spiritualize" its message—to somehow try to extract its wisdom and insight from its very specific and often peculiar demands. But the nature of a rule for community is that it cannot be read honestly as a guide for my "personal spiritual journey." To listen to it at all is to consider how it is telling me to pray and eat with other people; to submit my personal decisions to someone else's judgment; to invite strangers into my home; and to call nothing my own (even if I did work for it). This *Rule* was written to structure a shared life.

At the same time, this *Rule* contains within it a flexibility that invites translation. As specific as its instructions often are, it also goes out of its way to say that things might be done otherwise if conditions require it or if a community's leadership thinks it best.

Benedict was aware that he was applying a wisdom tradition to a specific context, and that it might apply differently in another time or place. Those communities that have lived the *Rule*[1] through the centuries and continue to do so today are concrete reminders of the way that the translation process Benedict engaged in must be continued in every generation. It's not enough to render the words of the *Rule* into the vernacular. An ongoing effort must be made to translate its ideas into the current context. The only way to read it faithfully is to let it re-shape your life.

This paraphrase aims to say in Benedict's voice what he might say to communities today. That we are all caught up in a transition similar to the one in which Benedict lived makes his *Rule* especially important for our time. But a common situation in history, while it might make the *Rule* an interesting study for us, does not itself recommend it as a guide. The authority of this *Rule* depends on the witness of Benedict and those who came before and after him—women and men who've helped the world see more clearly what it means to become truly human in the way of Jesus. That is to say, people throughout history have turned to *The Rule of Saint Benedict* for the same reason that people in sixth-century Italy flocked to Benedict himself: they saw a way of life that made sense and offered real hope.

---

1. This would include all those who call themselves by the name *Benedictine*, including the historic Roman Catholic monastic communities of the Order of St. Benedict, the Congregation of Cluny, the Cistercians, and the Trappists, but also "Benedictine" religious orders within the Anglican and Protestant churches. In addition, in our new century, many of the intentional religious communities known as neomonastic take inspiration from the Benedictines.

This, then, is my prayer for this paraphrase: may it stir in you a passion for the promises of the gospel life; may it challenge you to leave old habits behind; may it help you see what it could mean to share real life with God and other people where you are; may it catch you up in God's movement and make us all a people of light in dark days. Amen.

THE RULE OF SAINT BENEDICT

PROLOGUE

L isten, my child. I want you to place the ear of your heart on the solid ground of the Master's wisdom (what I received, I'm passing on to you). This advice is from a spiritual father who loves you and gives you the sort of counsel that will shape your whole life. Listening is hard work, but it's the essential work. It opens you up to the God that you've rejected when you have only listened to yourselves. If you're ready to give up your addiction to yourself, this message is for you: to listen is to equip yourself with the best resources available to serve the real Master, Christ the Lord.

For starters, begin every good work with this prayer: "Lord, bring it to completion." Since God is full of goodness and has already called us his children, we shouldn't grieve him by doing wrong. Instead, we should take advantage of the good gifts God has given us and become good listeners. This way we won't make God into an "angry father" or a "harsh task master" who punishes us for not following him to glory.

So, let's go! The Scriptures are stirring us, like fire in our bones: *It is high time now for you to wake from sleep* (Romans 13:11b). Let's open our eyes wide to the light that shines out from God, and open our ears to the voice from heaven that shouts out every day: *O that today you would hearken to his voice!* (Psalm 95:7b). And, again: *You who have ears to hear, listen to what the Spirit says to the churches* (Revelation 2:7). What does the Spirit say? *Come, children, listen to me, I will teach you the fear of the Lord* (Psalm 34:11). *Run while you have the light* of life, *lest the darkness* [of death] *overtake you* (John 12:35).

The Lord calls out to his worker in the midst of a crowd: *Is there anyone here who wants real life and longs for abundance here and now?* (Psalm 34:12). If you hear the call and your heart cries, "Yes!" then God speaks these words to you: If you want the good life that lasts forever, *keep your tongue from evil and your lips from lying. Turn from evil and do good; seek peace and pursue it* (Psalm 34:13–14). Once you all have done this, the Lord says: "*I'll keep my eye on you, and I'll hear every prayer; even before you ask me, I will say* [to you], *Here I am*" (Isaiah 58:9). My brothers and sisters, what is more delightful than to hear this voice of our Master calling to us? See how the Lord in his love shows us the way to real life! Putting on the uniform of faith and good works, let's set out on this way with the gospel as our guide. Let's chase after the King who has called us to his kingdom.

We will never be able to live out our days in the household of this King unless we run ahead by doing good works. But let us ask the Lord as the psalmist did: *Who can stay in your dwelling place, Lord; and who will find rest on your holy mountain?* (Psalm 15:1). After this question, listen closely to what the Lord says. He is showing us the very way to come and live with him when he writes: *One who walks blamelessly and does what is right; who speaks the truth from his heart and does not slander with his tongue; who has not wronged his neighbors nor listened to lies about them* (Psalm 15:2–3). This one has overcome the devil at every turn, turning his back on him and his temptations—keeping them far away from his heart. While these bad thoughts were still sprouting, he grabbed hold of them and dashed them against the rock that is Christ (cf. Psalm 137:9).

Note this: people who dwell in the household of God *fear the Lord* (Psalm 15:4). They do not get overly excited about their own good works. They know it is the Lord's power—not their own—working good in them. They praise the Lord, as the psalmist says: *Not to us, Lord, not to us, but to your name alone give glory* (Psalm 115:1). In the same way, the apostle Paul refused to take credit for the power of his preaching. He declared: *By God's grace I am who I am* (1 Corinthians 15:10a). And, again: *Whoever boasts should boast in the Lord* (2 Corinthians 10:17). This is also why the Lord says in the Gospel of Matthew: *Whoever hears these words of mine and does them is like a wise man who built his house on a rock; the floods came and the winds blew and beat against the house, but it did not fall—its foundation was solid stone* (7:24–25).

With this altar call, our Lord concludes his Sermon on the Mount, waiting for us to put it into action. So, you see, our whole life is a gift of the truce God has declared—a chance for us to relearn the life we were made for. As Saint Paul says: *Don't you know that the whole point of God's patience is to give you time to change?* (Romans 2:4b). All the while, the Lord assures us of his love: *I don't want sinners to die; I'm dying for them to turn back to me and live* (Ezekiel 33:11).

Brothers and sisters, we've asked the Lord who can live with him, and he has shown us how we can. Life with God is possible—but only in the way that God has shown us. We must get ready then— heart, mind, and spirit—for the great struggle of learning to listen to God's word. For what we cannot do in our own strength, let's ask the Master for the help of his grace. If we want to find the life that's really life (and not simply a way of postponing death), then let's run on while there's still time to accomplish these things by the light of life. Let's start to do now those things that will benefit us forever.

This is why we want to establish a school for the Lord's service. In drawing up its code of conduct, we hope to avoid anything harsh or burdensome. Even so, the good of everyone involved may compel us to establish some rules that seem strict. Know that it's not for the sake of the rules, but rather it is to help heal our brokenness and to safeguard our love. Don't be overwhelmed by fear and run away from the way that leads to salvation. It's bound to be hard at first, but as we move on in this way of life and in faith, we will run on the road of God's good words—our hearts overflowing with delight. We'll know what it means to live in the way of love, even if there are no words to describe it.

This, then, is our resolve: to never turn away from the Lord's teaching, but to put every good word of his into practice, sticking with our brothers and sisters in community until we die. Such patience, we know, will lead us to share in Christ's sufferings, but we trust it will also make us worthy to share in his kingdom. Amen.

REAL LIFE WITH GOD

Scholars who've studied the sources of St. Benedict's *Rule* tell us that this prologue is based on the early church's teaching in preparation for baptism. The way of life that Jesus revealed—the possibility of real life with God—was passed down through a process called catechesis (literally, "to make hear, instruct"). What the disciples first heard from Jesus, they learned to live out with their whole lives. When they were old, they passed this wisdom on in the only way it could be taught—by living and talking with disciples in the community that is Christ's body. Catechism is how the way of Jesus was passed from one generation to the next.

Benedict's *Rule*, then, is itself a kind of catechism. Even though it's been the central guidebook for Western monasticism, its vision of life isn't just for a particular sect of Christians called "monks" and "nuns." This is a vision for the whole world, rooted in a particular way of life. From the very start, Benedict lays out a vision of real life for all who want to live well. It's a vision that assumes that the Old and New Testaments reveal the bedrock truth about what it means to be human. It's a vision that trusts that we've seen the human being fully alive in Jesus Christ. But it's a fundamentally practical vision for all people.

The vision, in short, is this: left to our own desires, we make a mess of our lives. But our Creator has shown us the way to true life. To receive the gift of this way is to follow it. This is not a rule for some part of our life called "spiritual." It is a rule for all of life.

CHAPTER 1

Four Types of Monastics

Four kinds of people try to focus their whole lives on God: first, those who live together in monastic community, where they submit themselves to a rule of life and to the community's leadership.

Second, there are the solitaries whose souls have been well formed by the trials of community life. They've gotten beyond the initial excitement of monastic life and are, thanks to the help of their communities, ready to wrestle the devil on their own. Having come up through the ranks in their training, they're ready to do battle on the front lines, like the Desert Fathers and Mothers. Stable in their own faith, they're ready to stand with nothing but God's help. They no longer need their sister or brother to remind them what God's love looks like at every moment. They are prepared to face their own twisted desires and bad thoughts in solitude.

Third, there are the idealists who live in communities, neither listening to the wisdom of their sisters and brothers nor submitting to a rule that could purify them *as gold is purified by fire* (Proverbs 27:21). They are the worst kind, really. Their character is as soft as lead. Everything they do is driven by their own desires, so they lie to God when they call themselves "Christian communities." Two or three share a house together—or are even scattered about, not under the same roof—and their utopian experiments are their own projects, not the Lord's. The rule they follow is their own desires; they do whatever they like. If they believe something or choose it for themselves, that's their "rule"; if there's anything they don't like, they reject it as evil.

Fourth, and finally, there are the spiritual consumers who wander around from one place to another, visiting a community here, a conference there, always looking for the next best thing. They're always on the go, never settling down because they've become captive to their own desires and big ideas about what a life with God should look like. To tell the truth, they're worse than the hypocrites living in communities.

It's better to just stop than to go on and on about these different kinds of so-called "monastics" and their embarrassing way of life. Let's leave this typology behind, then, and with the help of the Lord move on to make a plan for the best kind of monastics—those sisters and brothers who long for an ordered life in Christ.

LONGING FOR COMMUNITY

While a longing for community—a desire for real relationship with God and other people—may bring us to monastic wisdom, the wisdom itself pushes back against our desires, suggesting that our longings are not enough. Benedict knows that a simple desire for community will not create healthy community. In fact, our hopes and dreams about community may be our greatest obstacle to true fellowship with others.

Marketing firms today understand that "community" sells, because people want it. They don't tell us how carbonated sugar water will help us or even how good it tastes. They show us pictures of people enjoying life together while holding cans of the drink they want us to buy. But we know that community is more than a soda shared with friends. We still haven't found what we're looking for.

Benedict knows that we need a better way forward. Community can't be based on our own best ideals. It can't be reduced to seven easy steps. God is not a means by which we can achieve our ideals; other people don't want to be a means either. The key to life together, Benedict sees, is learning to submit our own desires to the reality of others' needs and to God's direction for what life should look like. This is why, from the very beginning of the *Rule*, listening is the essential work. This way of life is shaped around learning to listen to God and to other people. "Listen, my child," the *Rule* begins. And it keeps whispering the same wisdom to us, again and again.

Leadership in Community

To be worthy of the task of leadership in community, an abba or amma should always remember what their title signifies by acting as a true parent should. The abba holds the place of Christ in the community since he is addressed by the title that Paul uses in Romans: *You have received the spirit of adoption by which we exclaim, "Abba, Father!"* (Romans 8:15b).

So the community's leader must never teach or ask anything that would deviate from the teachings of our Lord. Instead, every instruction, like the yeast of divine justice, should spread through the minds of the community's members. Let the abba always remember that at the final accounting, not only his teaching, but also his community's actions will be examined. An amma must always remember that she serves as manager under the Lord, and she will be responsible when the true CEO finds that the workers have not been doing their best. Still, if a manager has faithfully attended to workers who won't listen and tried her hardest to cure their unhealthy habits, she's done her job. She won't be charged for their debt when the balance sheet doesn't add up. She will be able to say to the Lord: *I've not kept your justice hidden away; I have proclaimed your truth and your salvation* (Psalm 40:10a), *but they have rebelled against me* (Isaiah 1:2d). Then the rebellious workers will have to face the consequence of choosing death over the gentle way God offered through the amma's instruction.

Anyone who is called "amma" or "abba" should lead their community with both good teaching and good living, pointing their members to the good way more by example than by words. Those who are willing to listen can receive God's commandments, but those who are stubborn need to see love lived out—even in the face of their stubbornness. If the abba says something should not be done, he better not do it himself *so that after preaching to others he won't be disqualified* (1 Corinthians 9:27b). He doesn't want to hear God calling to him in his sin: *How is it that you recite my laws and take my covenant on your lips when you hate discipline and toss my words behind you* (Psalm 50:16–17)? Or this: *How is it that you can see the splinter in your neighbor's eye but never notice the plank in your own eye* (Matthew 7:3)?

The leader of a community should always avoid favoritism. She shouldn't love one member more than another, unless she finds that someone is in fact better at listening and doing good. A well educated, middle-class person should not have a higher rank in the community than a poor person, except for some reason other than their social class. But the amma is free, if she has good reason, to change anyone's position in the community for the sake of justice. Still, all other things being equal, everyone should keep her normal position because *whether slave or free . . . we are all one in Christ* (Galatians 3:28b) and every worker deserves her pay in the Lord's company, for *God is not a respecter of persons* (Romans 2:11). The only things that make us stand out in God's eyes are good works and real humility. This is why the community's leader loves every member the same and applies the same rules to all, according to what their actions deserve.

When teaching, an abba should heed Paul's advice when he says: *Use argument, appeal, and correction* (2 Timothy 4:2b). His approach isn't always the same, but changes with the circumstances—sometimes arguing, sometimes encouraging; sometimes as stern as a drill sergeant, sometimes tender, as only a father can be with his child. With those who are rebellious and restless, he'll argue firmly; with those who listen and are patient and teachable, he will appeal for greater virtue; but as for those who are careless and stubborn, we give him full authority to confront their error and correct it. He should not overlook the sins of those who go astray, but should address them just as quickly as he can, as soon as he notices them. Never forget the fate of Eli, the priest at Shiloh, whose leadership was ruined by the sins of his sons (1 Samuel 2:11–4:18). For members who are in good standing and paying attention, the abba's first and second warnings should be verbal; but for those who are stubborn and at odds with everyone, he has to make the consequences clear from the very first offense. We have it on good authority that *the fool cannot be corrected with words* (Proverbs 29:19a), and again: *Strike your son with a rod and you will free his soul from death* (Proverbs 23:14).

An amma should always remember who she is and what she is called to, aware that more will be expected from the one to whom much has been entrusted. She has to be aware of the immensity of her task: she is directing souls on their way toward God, serving a variety of temperaments in the way they're best able to receive direction—coaxing, correcting, and encouraging—depending on what each individual needs. She must so accommodate herself to each person's needs that she will not only keep the community from falling apart, but will genuinely rejoice in the growth of each person. More than anything else, she must not be distracted by logistical details and management issues, stealing time from the dear children who are her primary responsibility. She should remember that her job description is Chief of Soul Care. This is the work she must account for at her annual review. And if she's tempted to say, *I didn't have the resources I needed to do the job well*, she should recall this verse: *Seek first the kingdom of God and his righteousness, and all other things will be given to you as well* (Matthew 6:33), and again, this one: *Those who fear the Lord lack nothing* (Psalm 34:9b).

The community leader has to know that anyone taking responsibility for souls should be ready to give an account for them. However many members are in the community, the leadership will have to account for each of them when it's time to give a report to God—all that in addition to answering for themselves. This is how a leader is constantly reminded to care for his own soul: by attending to others' conditions like a good doctor and constantly teaching them how to overcome their own hang-ups. In this way, he also learns how to treat the sickness in his own soul.

CHAPTER 3
Community Meetings

W henever there's something important to do in the community, the abba or amma should call an all-members meeting. The community leader's job is to explain the business; the community's job is to listen and say what seems right to them. After such a clarification of thought, the leader can determine the best way forward.

But it's important to call everyone together for counsel, because the Lord often reveals the best course through the most inexperienced member. The job of every member is to express their opinion with humility, not insisting that everyone see things the way she does. The decision belongs to the community leader—not so much because she's always right, but because it's important for every member to learn to listen. But just as it's important for a disciple to learn to listen to his teacher, it's also essential for the teacher to always be fair and reasonable in her decisions.

Whatever the situation, everyone is committed to follow the teachings of the *Rule*—leader and members alike. In the community no one rushes off to do what feels right without listening to the counsel of others. While disagreements will happen, no member should take his disagreement with leadership outside the community to stir up trouble. If anyone does, they should be subject to the community's discipline as outlined in the *Rule*. Always remember, leadership must submit to God and to the *Rule* in everything they do. Ammas and abbas know without a doubt that they have to give an account to God, the most just judge there is.

For less important business, community leaders can feel free to check in with just a few wise members. But it's always good to hear from someone else. That's why the Scripture says: *Do everything with counsel, and you won't be sorry after the fact* (Sirach 32:24).

WHY WE NEED LEADERS

Most people today are skeptical of institutions and cynical about leadership. Politicians make promises they don't intend to keep. CEOs serve their investors at all costs with little incentive to take care of workers or promote the common good. Even pastors are often caught up in sex scandals or money-making schemes. Those who are most eager to find an alternative to the selfish power-grabbing of our culture are often the most anti-institutional. In response to bad leadership, some think we'd do better with no leadership at all.

My selection of words and phrases from the corporate world is deliberate in this chapter. Benedict's wisdom is helpful, for he saw clearly that the point of leadership in community isn't so much to get things done as it is to offer a specific context for learning to listen. The problem with a culture where everyone is grabbing for power is that no one is able to submit to another and hear the voice of God.

The answer to our problem is not for everyone to listen to himself. Our selves, after all, are each already shaped by the twisted desires of the culture around us. This is why, however noble their hopes, Benedict is convinced that the spiritual seekers and communal dabblers have little chance of growing into the fullness of what God wants them to be. Our only hope is for our twisted selves to be reformed by submission to a rule and refined by the fire of relationships with other people to whom we belong. Whether that happens in a marriage, in a congregation, or in a monastic community, this reshaping of our desires is what life with God is all about. As St. Augustine said, only when we have been remade by grace can we "love God and do what we want."

The Tools for Good Works

I n the craft of life with God, we need tools to work with. Most of all, keep this tool close at hand: *Love the Lord your God with all your heart, with all your soul, and with all your might . . . and love your neighbor as yourself* (Matthew 22:37–39). And never let these get buried too deep in the tool box: *Do not kill, and do not commit adultery . . . neither steal nor long for what belongs to someone else* (Romans 13:9a); *do not give a false report about anything* (Matthew 19:18d). *Respect everyone* (1 Peter 2:17a), *and never do to someone else what you wouldn't want done to yourself* (Matthew 7:12).

Leave your own will behind so you can follow Christ (cf. Matthew 16:24); *put your body into training* (cf. 1 Corinthians 9:27); don't cater to your every desire, but love fasting as an opportunity to rush ahead in your pursuit of Christ. Use the extra time and resources you have to assist the poor, *to clothe the naked, to visit the sick* (Matthew 25:36a), to bury the dead. If someone is in trouble, help them. If someone is sad, comfort them.

You should not live the same way other people do; for you, the love of Christ takes first place. You don't lash out in anger or nurse a grudge against someone who's wronged you (no, you've learned a better way to deal with the trials that everyone faces). Don't fool yourself. When you greet someone with the peace of Christ, mean it! Don't avoid someone who needs to receive God's love through you. Make promises you can keep, always telling the truth to yourself even as you're honest with others.

Don't fight like other people fight, *returning evil for evil* (1 Thessalonians 5:15a). Instead, suffer patiently, refusing to pass another's violence on to someone else. *Love your enemies* (Matthew 5:44). If someone cusses you out, don't strike back with your own assault of words. Find a way to bless them instead. *Endure persecution for the sake of justice* (cf. Matthew 5:10).

Don't be addicted to your own self-image or to anything else that promises cheap fulfillment or an easy escape from problems. Beware of too much eating or too much sleeping. *Watch out for laziness* (Romans 12:11a). Don't spend your time complaining or talking bad about other people.

Put your hope in God alone. If you notice yourself doing good (that is the point, after all), give God all the credit. You're not doing it on your own. But you can be sure of this: whatever bad habits you hold onto, you get all the credit for those. It's up to you to acknowledge them and make amends.

If you're honest with yourself, you'll tremble at the thought of meeting God face-to-face and shudder when you consider God's judgment. Let that holy fear stir up your desire for living that life that's really life. Never forget: you are going to die. Every single thing you do is infinitely important, because God sees every act, no matter where you are. The moment you have a bad thought, dash it against Christ (he is a solid rock) and confess it to your spiritual director. Don't let a lie or a mean word cross your lips, but speak carefully, avoiding useless talk and the sort of jokes that stir up the worst in people.

Here's what you should do with every spare moment you have: listen to the wisdom of those who've gone before you and devote yourself to prayer. Take time to confess your sins to God every day—not just naming them, but taking time to grieve the great harm they've done to you and the whole universe. In your tears resolve to leave your addictions and protective mechanisms behind.

Don't give into your twisted desires (Galatians 5:16b); despise that voice that whispers, "Do what *you* need to do." Listen instead to the leadership of your community even if their actions (God forbid) don't match up with their advice. Remember what our Lord said about the Pharisees: *Do what they say, not what they do* (Matthew 23:3a).

There's no sense acting like you've achieved sainthood. Instead, work on becoming a saint in every little thing you do so your actions might one day speak for themselves. Make God's good words your constant guide: treasure chastity; don't harbor hatred or jealousy; and don't let envy drive a single action. Don't get into arguing, and turn your back on arrogance. Respect the wise and love the inexperienced in community. Out of love for Christ, say a prayer for the one who's become your enemy. If you have an argument with someone during the day, make peace with him before the sun goes down.

Last of all: never lose hope in God's mercy.

These are the tools of the spiritual craft that I want to pass on to you as a master carpenter passes his toolbox on to an apprentice. If we use them day and night, never laying them aside or getting distracted from our task, then we'll be able to return them to the true Master Carpenter when we meet him face-to-face. Our wages will be the reward he has promised: *What the eye has not seen nor the ear heard . . . God has prepared for those who love him* (1 Corinthians 2:9).

The workshop where we put all these tools to constant use is the community where God has called us to stay put.

LIFE WITH GOD AS CRAFT

Benedict knows that the wisdom he has to convey isn't the sort of information that you can cram in your memory for a multiple-choice test. It's more like woodworking than multiplication tables. While Scripture gives us words of instruction to describe a life with God, we learn that by walking it in the company of others. Like the master carpenter who shows an apprentice his tools and then stands beside him as he learns to use them, Benedict introduces tools for life with God to the disciple who is going to stay put in community, learning the craft from others. Apart from life together, these tools are as useless as a hammer might be to the son of a carpenter who makes his living at a desk job. But in the context of a community, their relevance is crystal clear. These are the tools that make it possible for people to live together in the way of Jesus.

This way of naming life with God also helps us see more clearly what a problem sin is. Our twisted desires, selfish impulses, defense mechanisms, and bad habits are not simply a failure to "hit the mark" that humans aim for. Sin is not a weakness. It is a sickness that infects communities, destroying the fabric of life itself. My own insecurities can lead to harsh words; in response, someone else's defense mechanisms can give rise to bitterness or even rage. Sin means that, left to ourselves, we'll kill each other in community. But to know Jesus as our Savior is to know that Jesus takes our violence upon himself without passing it on to someone else. In short, he stops the cycle of retribution. Because he does this, we can live a different way in the world.

Listening

The first step of humility is to listen without delay. When we love Christ more than anything else, this becomes our natural reflex. Our reasons for listening may vary—we listen because of the promise we've made to God, or because we dread the hell of only listening to ourselves, or simply because we want to know the glory of the life that's really life. But whatever our immediate reason, listening without delay means we do what we're asked as quickly as if it were a direct request from God.

The Lord is talking about this kind of good listener when he says: *As soon as they heard me they listened and did what I asked* (Psalm 18:44a); and again, the Lord says to teachers; *Whoever listens to you, listens to me* (Luke 10:16a). Good listeners are quick to put aside their own concerns. They're not obsessed with what they want, but will lay down their own projects—leaving them unfinished. Because they're always ready to listen, their actions are determined by an authority other than themselves. As soon as the community has a need, they are ready to meet it in humble submission to God. In this way, the sharing of the need by one member and the meeting of it by another happen as if they were a single act.

It is love that compels good listeners in their pursuit of real life. This is why they're always eager to follow the way about which our Lord said: *Narrow is the road . . . that leads to life* (Matthew 7:14a). They don't live by their own best judgments, listening to the people they like and doing the things that seem best to them. Instead, they let the wisdom of a community and its leadership shape their decisions.

This is, after all, why they live in Christian community. If they have made this way of life their choice, they will also make this saying of our Lord their mantra: *I have not come to do my own will, but the will of the One who sent me* (John 6:38b).

But here is a word of caution: good listening only pleases God and builds up a community when we do what we're asked without rolling our eyes or dragging our feet. Half-hearted obedience won't cut it, even if we end up doing what we were asked to do at first. The key is to see that when we listen to our sisters and brothers, we're listening to Jesus, who said himself: *Whoever listens to you, listens to me* (Luke 10:16a). And then, we're not only to listen, but also to listen gladly, *for God loves a cheerful giver* (2 Corinthians 9:7c). If a community member listens grudgingly, complaining to someone as she's doing what she was asked to do—or even grumbling to herself—this can't please God, who surely hears everything. Her service isn't any good to her or to anyone else. Unless she changes her whole approach, grumbling and complaining will ruin her.

THE DANGER OF COMPLAINING

People do not stay very long in community, in a family, in a church, or in a workplace without realizing that they don't always want to do what others expect them to do. Everyone knows the feeling. And no one likes it. Standard wisdom in our society is that you shouldn't bottle up that feeling of resentment inside of you. You should let it out. We usually call this process *venting*. A lot of the conversations that happen over cups of coffee, exercise equipment, or text messages in our society is energized by our desire to air the wrongs that we perceive to have been done against us. It feels good, we like to say, to get all of that off of our chests.

But whether our complaint is bottled up inside or aired among trusted friends, Benedict knows that it is deadly. Complaining is the cancer that destroys community. Like Paul, who looks back to Israel's experience in the wilderness and cautions against murmuring in I Corinthians 10:10, Benedict knows from experience what the whole tradition attests: we cannot begin to love God and neighbor until we have first "died to self"—that is, until we have submitted our ego to the way that promises real life through self-giving love. That way is a way of humility, and we take the first step toward living it in our commitment to listen intently to others in community. What does this posture of listening look like? For starters, Benedict says, it means we stop complaining. This is the one thing that most often destroys community. We have a lot to unlearn before we can really begin to practice the *Rule*.

CHAPTER 6

On Not Talking

Let's heed the psalmist's wisdom: *I said, I'm committed to watch my words so I don't sin with my tongue. I've sealed my lips . . . I was silent and was humbled. I held my peace and didn't even speak good words* (39:1–2). So there are times when even a good word—a true word—is best left unsaid. If silence is sometimes better than good words, then we ought all the more to avoid complaining and the ruin that comes with it.

As a matter of fact, silence is so important to our formation in community that the teacher shouldn't invite even the mature disciple to speak too often, no matter how insightful or well-intentioned her comment may be, for Proverbs tell us: *In a flood of words you will drown in sin* (10:19); and, again: *The tongue holds the key to life and death* (18:21). When it's time to learn the way that our Lord has shown us, talking is the teacher's job. The job of the disciple is to keep silence and listen.

The same also applies when any member makes a request of the community and its leadership. He should watch his words and speak with all humility and respectful submission.

In no situation should any member ever use vulgar words or engage in gossip. Even senseless talk that aims only to get a laugh out of others must be avoided.

The default for a disciple is silence. When we stop talking, we become better listeners.

CHAPTER 7
Humility

Sisters and brothers, Holy Scripture calls to us, saying: *Whoever exalts himself will be humbled, and whoever humbles himself will be exalted* (Luke 14:11). And what it's saying to us is this: every attempt we make to "climb the ladder" is rooted in pride, that the Psalms teach us to shun when they say: *Lord, my heart is not exalted; I haven't turned up my nose at anyone, nor have I walked in the halls of power, hoping for a position higher than my own* (131:1). Why does the psalmist say he's done this? *If I didn't have a humble spirit, but were exalted instead, then you would treat me like a weaned child on its mother's lap* (131:2).

So, then, sisters and brothers, if we want to climb to the heights of humility—that is, if we want to rush up to the glory of heaven by way of humility here and now—then we have to learn to climb the ladder on which Jacob saw angels going up and coming down in his dream (cf. Genesis 28:12). This much is clear: the angels' ascending and descending is a sign to us that we go down when we try to exalt ourselves and we rise up by way of humility. Our ladder, then, is the life we're living right here and now. If we learn to humble ourselves, the Lord will raise us to heaven's glory. We might even say that our action and our contemplation are the two sides of this ladder. As our vocation is to climb, God has also given us rungs of discipline to help us learn humility one step at a time.

The first step of humility requires a person to keep the *fear of God always before his eyes* (Psalm 36:1) and never forget it. The climber's first task is always to recall every good word from God, keeping in mind that anyone who hates God will fall to his death, but all who fear God have real life that lasts forever waiting for them at the end of their climb. The climber reminds himself that God is watching from above and sees him every step of the way. So, too, he learns to watch himself at every hour, guarding against every bad thought or misguided action that might distract him from his climb.

The psalmist reminds us again and again that our thoughts are always present to God: *God searches hearts and minds* (7:9b), and: *The Lord knows human thoughts* (94:11). Again, the psalmist prays: *You know my thoughts from afar* (139:2b), and: *The thoughts of people should bring you praise* (76:10a). In order to guard herself against bad thoughts, the virtuous sister should always say to herself: *I will be blameless in God's sight if I guard myself from my own wickedness* (Psalm 18:23).

In truth, we can't chase after our own desires, for Scripture tells us: *Turn away from your desires* (Sirach 18:30b). And in the Lord's Prayer, also, we ask God that his *will be done* in us (Matthew 6:10b). It's important for us to learn not to do our own will since we dread what Scripture warns us against: *There are ways that seem right to most people, but in the end they lead to destruction* (Proverbs 16:25). What's more, we fear what Scripture says about those who ignore this: *They are corrupt, and their desires are wicked* (Psalm 14:1b).

When it comes to the things that our bodies long for, we need to trust that God is always with us. For we pray: *All my desires are known to you* (Psalm 38:9a). We have to watch out for those natural desires that distract us from God, for death crouches at the gate of pleasure. This is why Scripture tells us: *Don't pursue your lust* (Sirach 18:30a).

So, if *the eyes of the Lord are watching the good and the wicked* (Proverbs 15:3), if *the Lord constantly looks down from heaven to see whether anyone understands and seeks God* (Psalm 14:2), and if there are angels reporting our every action and thought to the Lord day and night, then we need to be on our toes at all times. Otherwise, as the psalm goes on to say, God may see us *falling into evil* and *ruining ourselves* (14:3a). Our God is a loving father who waits patiently for us to improve. But don't think that God's silence means he does not see. For one day, you may hear God say: *This you did, and I was silent* (Psalm 50:21a).

The second step of humility calls the climber to stop loving her own desires and no longer to find satisfaction in getting what she wants. Instead, she learns to imitate in her actions the saying of our Lord: *I have come not to do my own will, but the will of him who sent me* (John 6:38). This is why the holy martyr Saint Irene said, when she was threatened with forced prostitution, "To do this willingly would merit punishment, but to suffer it at your hands will earn me a crown."[2]

The third step of humility is submission. It teaches the climber to listen closely to the leadership of his community out of love for God, imitating our Lord, about whom Paul said: *He became obedient to death* (Philippians 2:8b).

The fourth step of humility is to listen and do what you are asked, even when it is difficult, inconvenient, or unjust—to quietly embrace suffering and to endure it without giving up or running away. For Scripture says: *Anyone who perseveres to the end will be saved* (Matthew 10:22b), and again: *Be strong and take heart! Trust in the Lord* (Psalm 27:14). Another passage shows us how God's faithful ones will endure anything for the Lord's sake, praying even as they suffer: *For your sake we face death all day long; we are counted as sheep marked for the slaughter* (Romans 8:36). They are so confident in God's promise to reward them that they sing on joyfully and shout: *But in all of this we are more than conquerors because of him who so*

2. St. Irene of Thessalonica, one of three sisters who were martyred for the faith in Macedonia in 304.

greatly loves us (Romans 8:37)! In the Psalms, which teach us how to sing faithfully, it says: *God, you have tested us; you have tried us as silver is tried in the fire. You led us into prison and made us carry a heavy load on our backs* (66:10–11). And then, to show that we should suffer in submission to someone who is over us, the psalmist also says: *You have placed other people over our heads* (66:12a).

The truth is that the people who are patient in the difficulties of community life—those who do not protest, even when they're treated unjustly—are fulfilling our Lord's command: *When struck on one cheek, they turn the other; when deprived of their coat, they offer the shirt off their own back; when drafted for one tour of duty, they voluntarily serve a second* (Matthew 5:39b–42). Along with the apostle Paul, they bear with *unfaithful community members, endure persecution, and bless those who curse them* (cf. 2 Corinthians 11:26; 1 Corinthians 4:12).

The fifth step of humility is to stop hiding bad thoughts and sinful actions that others don't see, and to bow your head and confess them to your amma or abba. This is what Scripture is talking about when it tells us: *Make your way known to the Lord and put your hope in him* (Psalm 37:5). And again: *Confess to the Lord, for he is good; his mercy endures forever* (Psalm 106:1). It's why the psalmist prays again: *To you have I acknowledged my offense; I haven't concealed my faults. I said: "Against myself I will report my faults to the Lord," and you have forgiven the wickedness of my heart* (32:5c).

The sixth step of humility is to be content to live as the least important person in your community—glad to wash the dishes or scrub the toilets—to say as the psalmist teaches us: *I am insignificant and ignorant, no better than a brute beast before you; yet, I am with you always* (73:22–23a).

The seventh step of humility is to not only say with your mouth but also believe in your heart that you are less important than everyone else. It is to bow down and pray with your whole being: *I am truly a worm, not a human being, scorned by others and despised by the people* (Psalm 22:6). *I was exalted, but then I was humbled and overwhelmed with confusion* (Psalm 88:15). And again: *It is a blessing that you have humbled me so that I can learn to listen to your good words* (Psalm 119:71).

The eighth step of humility is to do nothing other than what is given to you by the community's rule and by the example of older members.

The ninth step of humility is to choose your words carefully and learn to keep silent, only speaking when another is really ready to listen, for Scripture warns us: *In a flood of words you will drown in sin* (Proverbs 10:19a), and again: *The one who talks all the time doesn't know how to find her way on earth* (Psalm 140:11).

The tenth step of humility is not to laugh too easily, for it is written: *Only a fool raises his voice in laughter* (Sirach 21:23a).

The eleventh step of humility is to speak gently and without wisecracks, humbly and seriously, saying only the necessary and reasonable words, and never raising your voice. As it is written, "A wise man is known by his few words."[3]

The twelfth step is to let humility shape the way you carry yourself every bit as much as it shapes your thoughts, so that it makes a real difference in how you act at common prayer or out in the garden; when making a trip away from the community or when you're on the job.

---

3. Benedict is quoting the *Enchiridion* of Sextus Pythagoricus, a collection of proverbs he probably learned during his classical education.

Remember, every rung of the ladder connects prayer to action. Whether the climber is sitting, walking, or just standing around, humility should shape her whole posture. Since she is aware of her sin and weakness, she should always live as if she were before the Lord for the final reckoning, constantly praying in her heart the prayer that the publican said with downcast eyes: *Lord, I am a sinner, not worthy to look up to heaven* (Luke 18:13b). And, likewise, the psalmist's prayer: *I am bowed down and humbled in every way* (38:7).

So now, after ascending all these steps, the climber will quickly arrive at that *perfect love* of God *that casts out fear* (1 John 4:18a). What began with fear, then, will be transformed by God's love, so that the things the monastic first learns to do with fear and trembling she will then begin to do without effort, as though they were second nature. Fear is no longer the motivator, but rather love for Christ, good habit, and the delight that comes with living the life we were made for. All of this is possible because of the Lord, who works through the Holy Spirit to wash us clean from our bad habits and sins.

HUMOR AND HUMILITY

In many ways, Benedict's "Ladder of Humility" sums up the *Rule*. The whole point of faith is to move through prayer and action from a reverence for God's holiness to a celebration of God's love for all creation. The conclusion to chapter 7 echoes the great line from Abba Anthony the Great, the father of Christian monasticism: "I no longer fear God, but I love him."

This is a beautiful image of the human being fully alive, caught up in the eternal dance of God's life. To imagine the faces of a community so enraptured is inevitably to recall images of parties and celebrations. In almost all of those memories, there is the sound of laughter. Why, then, is laughter something Benedict cautions us so strongly against?

A young man who was attending junior high school in China when terrorists attacked The World Trade Center and Pentagon on September 11, 2001, tells the story of how he learned about the tragedy on his way to school that morning. When he got to class, all of his friends were talking about it. Some joked that the images on television were better than the video games they had at home. After the bell rang, the teacher walked into the classroom, looked at the kids, and said, "Laughter is a cheap substitute for grief." This young man never forgot those words.

Humor is one way humans negotiate the tension between the world that we hope for and the world that we dream of. Our best comedians often suffer from depression, because they see too clearly the distance between heaven and earth.

Yes, they know how to make us laugh. But at the end of the day, they don't know how to bridge the great chasm that threatens to swallow up everything dear to us.

Benedict's Ladder of Humility is a way of summing up God's invitation in Jesus for humanity to receive the gift of a bridge that can carry us from the life we know to the life that we were made for. It is a way, like grief, that does not simply jump over suffering, but goes through it, trusting that even our hardships can be redeemed. Laughter, Benedict seems to say, is a cheap substitute for this way of sorrowful joy. This doesn't mean that we don't have occasions to sing and dance—to laugh, even—on our way to glory. It simply means that we will not be distracted from the serious business of joy. We will not go for cheap substitutes. Our single focus is pressing on toward the life that is really life.

CHAPTER 8

On Rising Early for Prayer

During the winter, when the night is long, the community can go to bed early. This makes it easy to get up well before the sun—at 2 AM even—to begin praying while it is still dark. By sleeping a little past the middle of the night, the sisters and brothers can get up rested with their evening meal digested. After this vigil, while it is still dark, they can memorize psalms or practice holy reading.

In the summer, when night is shorter, the time for rising from bed should be adjusted to allow for rest. Allow enough time between Vigils and Morning Prayer to get ready for the day.

Morning Prayer should always be held just after daybreak.

CHAPTER 9
An Order for Vigils

During the winter, always begin Vigils with this verse: *Lord, open my lips and my mouth shall proclaim your praise* (Psalm 51:15). After saying this three times, follow this order: Psalm 3 with the *Gloria* ("Glory be to the Father, and to the Son, and to the Holy Spirit, as it was in the beginning, is now, and will be forever"), Psalm 95 with a refrain (or at least chanted), a hymn, then six psalms with a refrain.

After the psalms, the amma or abba sings a verse with a response from the community, then offers a blessing. When everyone is seated, members read three passages from the book that the community is reading together. After each reading, the community sings a response. The *Gloria* isn't sung after the first two, but always after the third. As soon as the community begins to sing "Glory be to the Father," everyone should stand in honor and reverence for the Holy Trinity.

In addition to readings from the Old and New Testament at Vigils, Christian classics by the saints whose wisdom we celebrate and recognize should be read.

After these three readings and their responses have been finished, the remaining six psalms are sung with an "alleluia" refrain. At the end of that cycle, everyone recites together a reading from the epistles of Paul that they have memorized; a call and response; and, finally, "Lord, have mercy." This concludes the order for Vigils.

CHAPTER 10
A Modified Order for Summer

During the winter, the above order is followed for Vigils. But because of the shorter nights in summer, the readings are omitted. In place of these three readings, one from the Old Testament is substituted. This should be recited by heart, followed by a short response. Otherwise, the winter order for Vigils should be kept. In that way, both winter and summer, there are never fewer than twelve psalms at Vigils, not counting Psalms 3 and 95.

CHAPTER 11
Special Instructions for Vigils on Sunday

On Sundays the sisters and brothers should rise earlier than normal for Vigils (every week, after all, is a Holy Week. We get up to greet our risen Lord!). But even at this most important vigil, we don't want to be too extreme.

First, as we've already said, six psalms are said, followed by a call and response. Then everyone can have a seat while we listen to four readings from the book. After each reading, a response is sung, saving the *Gloria* for the end. Again, as soon as the *Gloria* begins, we should stand up again in reverence.

After these readings, the same order is repeated: six more psalms with a refrain; a call and response; then four more readings and their responses, as before. After that, three passages from the prophets are said with an "alleluia" refrain. Then, after a call and response with the amma or abba's blessing, four New Testament readings follow with responses.

After the fourth response, the community leader leads the hymn: "We praise you, God." Then she reads from the Gospel while the whole community stands in respect and awe. At the conclusion of the Gospel reading, everyone says *Amen* and the amma sings: "To you be praise." After a final blessing, the community moves directly to Morning Prayer.

This arrangement for Vigils on Sunday should be followed all the time, summer or winter, unless—God forbid—the whole community happens to oversleep. In that case the readings and responses are the place to cut. Take special care to set an alarm and make sure this doesn't happen. But if it does, let the one who is responsible ask God for forgiveness in the place where the community gathers for prayer.

CHAPTER 12

Morning Prayer on Sundays

Sunday's Morning Prayer begins with Psalm 67, said straight through without a refrain. Then Psalm 51 follows, with an "alleluia" refrain.

Morning Prayer continues with Psalms 118 and 63; a hymn; Psalms 148 through 150; a reading from the Revelation, recited by heart with a sung response; another hymn; a call and response; Zechariah's song (Luke 1:68–79); and the litany in which we cry, "Lord, have mercy."

WHY WE RISE EARLY

Contemporary writer Annie Dillard writes that she rises early to write in the dark, because darkness is the place where "memory and imagination meet." Even in a modern urban setting, where people work three shifts a day, a certain stillness descends on most places by three or four in the morning. The invitation to Vigils is an invitation to begin our day with God in this time of quiet.

Every vigil is a reminder of the first Easter morning when women who loved Jesus went to his tomb to anoint his body. They did not know that Jesus was already risen—that death had been defeated, though it was still night. But they went in the quiet that comes before dawn to honor their Lord.

Vigils, then, is an invitation to honor God and sing praises before the light of dawn. It's an opportunity to come expectantly, even as we're longing for the world that is to be transformed into the world that ought to be. "We who believe in freedom cannot rest," as the old spiritual says. So we get up before dawn and saturate ourselves in the psalms that are the prayers of Jesus. And whatever extra time we have, we use to memorize those words and get them deep down inside of us. What Benedict knows is that these prayers make us into different people. We become the answer to the prayers we pray, as God's grace does its work on us in this school for conversion.

CHAPTER 13
Morning Prayer on Ordinary Days

On weekdays, Morning Prayer is said as follows: first, Psalm 67 is said without a refrain, but drawn out a bit to make sure everyone is there when Psalm 51, which does have a refrain, begins. Next, according to custom, two other psalms are added each day: Monday—Psalms 5 and 36; Tuesday—Psalms 43 and 57; Wednesday—Psalms 64 and 65; Thursday—Psalms 88 and 90; Friday—Psalms 76 and 92; Saturday—Psalm 143 and Deuteronomy 32:1–12, divided into two sections, with the *Gloria* sung after each. On other days, one of the songs of the prophets is sung, according to the tradition of the Roman church. Next follows Psalms 148–150 (psalms of praise, that give Morning Prayer the name *Lauds*); a reading from Paul (recited by heart); a response; a hymn; a call and response; Zechariah's song; the litany in which we cry, "Lord, have mercy," and the conclusion.

Make sure of this: Morning and Evening Prayer should never end without the community's leader reciting the entire Lord's Prayer for everyone to hear. We always pray, *forgive us . . . as we forgive*, because we know thorns of contention are bound to spring up in any human community. As we keep this reality always before us, we pray to be cleansed from the stain of unforgiveness. At other times, only *lead us not into temptation* is said aloud so that everyone may reply *but deliver us from evil* (Matthew 6:13).

CHAPTER 14

Special Instruction for Vigils on the Anniversary of a Saint

When celebrating a saint's day (or any other holy occasion, for that matter), the Sunday order is followed for Vigils. The only exception is that the psalms, refrains, and readings for that particular saint's day are said. The order stays the same as what is outlined above.

When to Say Alleluia in Prayers

Alleluia is the language of heaven, and it should be sung out with both the psalms and the responses from Easter until Pentecost. Let the celebration of Christ's resurrection resound at every gathering!

Then, from Pentecost until the beginning of Lent, *alleluia* is sung only with the last six psalms of the Vigil. Apart from Vespers, the last office, every office of prayer is said with the "alleluia" on Sundays, except during Lent. At Vespers, a refrain is used. But *alleluia* is never said during the call and response, except from Easter to Pentecost.

An Order for Prayers throughout the Day

The psalmist says: *Seven times a day have I praised you* (Psalm 119:164a). We, too, can keep the holy number seven if we set a schedule to follow Morning Prayer with two other offices before noon (*Prime* and *Terce*, to use the technical terms), then Midday Prayer, followed by a midafternoon office (*None*), an evening office, and the office of Compline before going to bed. These are the fixed times the psalmist was referring to when he said: *Seven times a day have I praised you.*

Concerning Vigils, which is really an eighth hour of prayer, the psalmist also says: *At midnight I arose to give you praise* (Psalm 119:62a). This is why we praise our Creator for his just judgments at the seven fixed hours and also rise early to give him praise.

The Number of Psalms to Sing at Each Hour

Since we've already set a schedule for psalms during the Vigil and Morning Prayer, it remains to arrange the psalms to pray during other offices:

- *Prime*—Three psalms, each followed by the *Gloria*. The hymn for this hour is sung right after *O God, come to my assistance*, before the psalms begin. Then, after the psalms, one reading follows and the hour is concluded with a call and response, "Lord, have mercy," and the dismissal.

- *Terce*, Midday, and *None*—the same order applies: the opening verse; the hymn appropriate for each hour; three psalms; a reading with a call and response, "Lord, have mercy," and the dismissal. If the community is large, refrains are used with the psalms; if not, the psalms are said without a sung response.

- Evening Prayer—four psalms, with refrain. After these psalms, a reading and response; a hymn; a call and response; Mary's Song; the litany; and, just before the dismissal, the Lord's Prayer.

- Compline—three psalms without refrain; then a hymn for this hour; a reading; a call and response; "Lord, have mercy"; a blessing and the dismissal.

CHAPTER 18
The Order of the Psalms

Each of the hours of prayer during the day begins with the verse: *God, come to my assistance; Lord, make haste to help me* (Psalm 70:1). This is followed by the *Gloria* and the appropriate hymn.

At *Prime* on Sunday, four sections of Psalm 119 are said. Then, throughout the other offices of the day, three sections of this same psalm are read at each prayer. On Monday, three psalms are said at *Prime*: 1, 2, and 6. At *Prime* each day thereafter, three psalms are said in consecutive order up to Psalm 20. In this way, Vigils on Sunday can always begin with Psalm 21.

On Monday, at *Terce*, Midday, and *None*, the remaining nine sections of Psalm 119 are said, three sections at each hour. In this way, Psalm 119 is completed in two days—Sunday and Monday. On Tuesday, three psalms are said at each of these hours, 120 through 128. These same psalms are repeated at these hours daily, Tuesday through Saturday, as are the hymns, readings, and call and response. This way, Psalm 119 will always begin on Sunday.

Four psalms are sung each day at Evening Prayer, starting with Psalm 110 and ending with Psalm 147, but skipping the psalms that are already assigned to other offices: 118–128, 134, and 143. All the remaining psalms are said at Evening Prayer. Since this leaves three psalms too few, the longest three should be divided: 139, 144, and 145. And because Psalm 117 is short, it can be said together with Psalm 116. This is the order of psalms for Evening Prayer. The rest of the office is arranged as outlined above.

The same psalms—4, 91, and 134—are said each day at Compline.

The psalms that are not otherwise accounted for in this arrangement for the daytime hours are distributed evenly at Vigils over the seven nights of the week. Longer psalms are divided so that twelve psalms are said each night.

If for any reason this arrangement doesn't work, a community should feel free to rearrange the psalms as needed, so long as all 150 psalms are said each week and the cycle begins again at Sunday's Vigil. Monastics who do not pray through the whole Psalter, along with the customary biblical songs, at least every week, show signs of being lazy and lacking devotion. After all, we read that the Desert Fathers and Mothers, full of zeal, prayed through the whole Psalter every day! Let's hope that we, weak as we may be, can at least get through it every week.

A SCHEDULE FOR PRAYER

Why does Benedict go to such great lengths to tell us exactly how to pray the psalms? After all, he says himself that another arrangement could work just as well, provided it doesn't leave any psalms out. The painstaking detail of these chapters is a reminder that conversation with God, however lofty or spiritual it may seem, comes down to details. When are we going to pray? Where? With whom? How?

People who go on retreat at a monastic community often comment how grounding it is to be part of a community that knows when to pray together. Most communities know that people have to eat and so establish regular intervals throughout the day to pause for meals. Yet, however spiritual we may be, most modern people don't set aside specific times of the day to stop and pray. Travel to a Muslim country, and the public call to prayer rings out as a peculiar interruption. Fixed-hour prayer is strange to most of us.

But a commitment to prayer that never gets down to the details of schedule is hardly a commitment at all. Though seven times a day is a goal with biblical resonance, we need not be put off by Benedict's apparent high standards. He is, after all, presenting a rule that is intentionally less harsh than those he inherited. The heart of the fixed-hour prayer tradition is morning, midday, and evening prayer. To begin and end our days in common prayer is a big step away from the individualism of contemporary spirituality and toward the kind of community with God and neighbor that Benedict imagined.

CHAPTER 19
How to Pray the Psalms

We believe that God is present everywhere and that *in every place the eyes of the Lord are watching the good and the bad* (Proverbs 15:3). If this is always true, how much more so when we're saying the divine hours of prayer?

This is why we have to always remember what the psalmist says: *Serve the Lord with fear* (Psalm 2:11a), and again: *Sing praise wisely* (Psalm 47:7b), and: *In the presence of angels I will sing to you* (Psalm 138:1b). The thing to consider at prayer, then, is how we ought to behave in the presence of God and his angels. We should stand to sing the psalms in such a way that our very being is in harmony with our voices.

CHAPTER 20
On Reverence at Prayer

If we want to ask a favor of an influential person, we do it with humility and respect, lest the important person think we're presuming too much of them. How much more important is it, then, for us to bring our requests before the Lord God with true humility and sincere devotion? God doesn't listen to our words as much as he sees the true intention of our hearts. This is why we should say short prayers, unless we're somehow inspired by God's grace to pray longer. But when bowing together as a community, we should always be brief. And when the leader gives the signal, everyone should stand together.

Group Leaders in the Community

If the community is large, some sisters or brothers who have a good reputation and are well formed in the way of Jesus should be chosen as group leaders. They will watch over groups of ten, managing everything according to the good words of God and the community's leadership. The group leaders should be the kind of people with whom the amma or abba can confidently share the responsibilities of leadership. They should be chosen according to their character and wisdom—not their rank.

If it happens that one of these group leaders succumbs to the temptation of pride, he should be corrected once, twice, and even a third time. But if he refuses to change, he should be removed from this position and replaced by another who can do the job. The same goes for anyone in leadership—the office is not more important than any one person's climb toward humility.

Arrangements for Sleeping in the Community

M onastics are to sleep in separate beds. They don't need fine linens and soft pillows, but should be given simple bedding by the community's leadership.

When it's possible, the whole community should sleep under the same roof. But if the community is too large, then monastics can sleep in groups of ten or twenty under the watchful care of a group leader. A night-light should be left on until morning.

Everyone should sleep in his clothes, though it's good for each person to empty his pockets so he doesn't poke himself when he rolls over. This way, the monastic will always be ready to get up when the signal is given for prayer. Each person will hurry to get to the Work of God before the others, but he won't do it haphazardly. They'll do it as if they're rushing to a meeting at the White House.

The younger members of a community shouldn't all sleep in the same house or the same part of a house. It's better to have mixed households where the old and the young live together. When they rise early for prayer, they will be able to encourage one another quietly. For we know that sleepyheads always have an excuse at that hour.

CHAPTER 23
Discipline in the Community

I f a community member digs in her heels and refuses to listen—
if she is always complaining or hates the community's way
of life and instructions from her elders—then she should be
warned twice by her amma or group leader, as our Lord taught
us in Matthew 18. If she doesn't change her ways, she must be
confronted before everyone at a community meeting. But
if she still does not change, then she must be cut off from the
community, provided she's able to understand that she's choosing
to face the world alone, without any support from the community
that loves her. If for some reason she's not able to understand this,
then it's better for her to undergo physical discipline. It's better to
try every possible way to wake a person up than to hand her over to
face the harsh realities of her choices on her own.

⤚ CHAPTER 24 ⤙
Degrees of Discipline

The severity of discipline ought to be in proportion to the seriousness of a community member's fault. It's the responsibility of the community's leadership to determine how severe a fault is.

If the fault is less severe, for example, then it may make sense to exclude the guilty member from table fellowship. Anyone who receives this punishment should not lead prayers until he has repented and been restored to the community. He should eat alone, after everyone else has eaten together. If the community eats lunch at noon, he will eat in the midafternoon; if the community members eat dinner at 6 PM, he'll get his at 7:30 PM until he's gone through the proper process of reconciliation.

CHAPTER 25
Serious Faults

If a fault is severe—if it ruptures the fabric of trust in community—then the member who committed it should be excluded from both table fellowship and common prayer. No one should associate or have a conversation with this member at all. He should do his work alone, living as a man of constant sorrows, thinking always about the judgment that Paul wrote about: *Such a person is handed over for the destruction of his flesh so that his spirit may be saved on the day of the Lord* (1 Corinthians 5:5). He must eat alone, and only what the community's leadership considers appropriate for him to eat. He should not be blessed when members pass him in the hall, nor should the food that is sent for him be blessed.

CHAPTER 26
The Danger of Not Affirming the Community's Discipline

If someone in the community decides to reach out to the member who's been cut off from fellowship without permission—if he tries to have a side conversation or to slip him a note—he should receive a like punishment and also be cut off.

Care for the Member Who Has Been Cut Off

The community's leaders must pour out all their energy, and exercise their best pastoral gifts to care for the wayward member, because *it is not the healthy who need a doctor, but the sick* (Matthew 9:12). They should use every skill of a wise doctor and send in "specialists"—that is, wise and mature members who can support the wavering member, even as he continues to face the harsh possibility of a life cut off from those who love him the most. These specialists should urge him to be humble, as a way of working toward reconciliation, and they should console him *lest he be overwhelmed by excessive sorrow* (2 Corinthians 2:7b). For Paul also says: *Let love for him be reaffirmed* (2 Corinthians 2:8). So everyone should pray for him.

But the leaders are responsible for putting the community's prayer into action. They must act with all speed, discernment, and diligence so as not to lose a single sheep from their flock. Their job is to care for the sick, not to badger the healthy. So every leader should remember this condemnation of bad leadership: *What you saw to be fat you claimed for yourselves, and what was weak you cast aside* (Ezekiel 34:3a–4a). The leader should imitate the loving example of the Good Shepherd who left the ninety-nine sheep who were safe on the hillside to search for the one that had wandered off. His compassion for that one lost sheep was so great that he mercifully placed it on his sacred shoulders and so carried it back to the flock (cf. Luke 15:5).

CHAPTER 28
On Those Who Refuse to Change

If a member has been confronted time and again for the same fault, or if he has even been cut off for a time, but still hasn't changed his ways, then he needs something else—a form of discipline that can shake him from his sleep. Every good doctor knows that the best treatment can sometimes hurt the worst. Still, there's no guarantee that the treatment will work.

If, God forbid, the patient gets worse—if he becomes proud and tries to defend his actions—the good doctor must go through the whole course, applying compresses, the ointment of encouragement, the medicine of Holy Scripture, and finally the cauterizing iron of harsh discipline.

But if, even after all of this, the good doctor can see that his efforts are not working, he should resort to an even better remedy: he and the whole community should pray for the wayward member so that the Lord, who can do all things, may miraculously send healing.

If even this procedure does not work, then finally the good doctor must use his knife and amputate. For Paul does say: *Banish the evil one from among you* (1 Corinthians 5:13b), and again: *If the unbeliever departs, let him depart* (1 Corinthians 7:15a), so that one diseased sheep might not infect the whole flock.

Welcoming Back the One Who Has Left

If a member does persist in his own evil ways and leaves the community, but later wants to come back, he must first promise to make full amends for leaving. Welcome him back, but as a test of his humility welcome him once again as a novice. If he leaves again, or even a third time, it should be the same every time he comes back: he starts again as if for the first time. But after a third time, he needs to understand that if he leaves again, he cannot come back.

How to Correct Young Members

Discipline should always be age-appropriate. If a member is too young to understand the seriousness of being cut off from community, then his faults should be addressed with more immediate consequences so that he may be healed.

DISCIPLINE IN COMMUNITY

When we talk about discipline in today's world, it's usually in the context of raising kids. Parents think about how to help their children understand consequences and become responsible adults. Schools have to figure out how to deal with discipline problems, so that everyone is safe and able to learn. But the assumption is that our children will learn self-discipline—and the sooner the better. We are increasingly a society that simply locks behind bars those who cannot flourish as self-disciplined individuals.

This set of assumptions makes Benedict's eight chapters on discipline in community life seem particularly strange. Yes, he has called the monastic community a "school for the Lord's service." But does he really think that adults can (or should) submit to eating alone or not fellowshipping with others because of some fault that someone else has identified in his life? We're prone to feel that Benedict is proposing a community that runs like an elementary school class.

Yet, if we listen closely, it is clear that these instructions grow out of experience. Benedict has, indeed, led communities of responsible adults. He knows something about our tendency to serve ourselves, even when we've declared our intentions to be otherwise. He seems to have special insight into a principal struggle of the modern soul: namely, addiction.

The problem with addiction—whether to an illegal substance or to illusions about ourselves—is that it blinds us to the consequences of our own actions. We cannot discipline ourselves precisely because we cannot see ourselves truthfully. A life with others is inevitably a life in which we must learn the difficult truth of what our life looks like to someone else. Whether that happens in a marriage, a friendship, a congregation, or a community, the way forward from such a difficult realization will be an acknowledgment that our own good depends on submitting to the wisdom of another's perspective. That is the gift of discipline.

Qualifications of the Business Manager

Every community needs a business manager. Someone should be chosen from the ranks who is wise, mature, and careful, not gluttonous, proud, excitable, offensive, or wasteful. She should, instead, be God-fearing, and serve as a mother to the whole community. She will take care of everything, but will not run things her own way—she'll listen closely to the community's leadership.

She should not hassle community members. If anyone happens to make an unreasonable request of her, she should not back her off with a strong reaction, but reasonably and humbly explain why she cannot do what is asked. Let her watch over her own soul, always remembering what Paul says: *Whoever serves well secures a good place for himself* (cf. 1 Timothy 3:13).

She must always take care of sick members, children, guests, and the poor, knowing for sure that she'll answer at the final reckoning for how she treated them. She will handle the community's pots and pans, furniture and supplies, like a priest handles the sacred vessels at the altar, careful not to neglect anything. She should not be greedy, neither wasteful or extravagant with the community's resources, but should do everything with moderation, according to the direction of the community's leadership.

More than anything else, let her be humble. If she does not have resources to supply what someone asks for, let her at least offer kind words in response, for it is written: *A kind word is better than the best gift* (Sirach 18:17). She should take care of everything entrusted to her, and not presume responsibility for things the community has not asked her to manage.

She will provide community members with the food that is allotted for each of them without any pride or delay, so as not to distract anyone from their task. She should always remember what Scripture says about the one *who leads one of the little ones astray* (Matthew 18:6a).

If the community is large, she should be given helpers so she can calmly carry out the duties assigned to her. Whatever is necessary should be requested and provided at the proper time so that no one is agitated or distressed in the house of God.

CHAPTER 32
The Community's Property

The community's leadership should entrust all property—tools, clothes, cars, computers—to members whom they can trust. Whatever is needed should be checked out and returned after use, such as books at a library. Leadership is responsible for keeping good records, as a librarian would, so that when the members transition from one job to another everyone knows where to find what's needed.

Anyone who doesn't take good care of the community's property should be confronted by the leadership. If he doesn't change his ways, then he should be subjected to the discipline outlined above.

The Danger of Private Ownership

More than anything, the evil weed of private ownership must be uprooted and torn out of the community. Without instructions from leadership, no one should give, receive, or keep anything as her own—not a laptop, not a book, not even a pencil. Nothing can be claimed as our own since we have given up control of even our bodies and wills. Like Jesus, we look to our father (that is, our amma or abba) to provide all of our needs. We don't accept anything except what is allotted to us by these spiritual parents. *Everything should be the common possession of everyone*, as it is written, so that *no one calls anything his own* (Acts 4:32).

If anyone is caught nurturing this dangerous weed, he should be warned—not once only, but twice. If it happens a third time, he must be disciplined. This weed has to be rooted out.

CHAPTER 34
Sharing according to Need

That great passage from Acts continues: *Distribution was made to each according to his need* (4:35). This doesn't mean that we ever play favorites (God forbid!), but that the community should consider a member's weaknesses. Whoever needs less should thank God and not worry about someone else getting more. But if a member really does need more, she should be humbled by her weakness, not puffed up by her advantage, as if the leadership were giving her preferential treatment. In this way, everyone can be at peace.

Be sure of this: whatever happens, there must not be a word—not even a sign—of complaining. No matter the injustice (perceived or actual)—we can't let this weed get a foothold. If anyone is caught complaining, he should be disciplined with even greater seriousness. For complaining will destroy a community in no time.

DEALING WITH STUFF

Gandhi is well known for his renunciation of private property. Like Francis of Assisi before him, Gandhi saw the deep connection between ownership and violence. But Gandhi's friends often said to him, "your poverty costs us a great deal!" They saw what Benedict knew: even when we turn from the love of money, we still have to find a way to deal with stuff.

These chapters on the business affairs of a community are rich with insight both into the practical necessities of life together and into the individual temptations that we each face. Benedict recognizes, among other things, that "simplicity" does not mean the same thing for everyone. He is sensitive to the ways that class difference creates different expectations and even abilities in people. It's good, he says, to have learned how to live with less. (The poor, then, have a certain advantage in God's upside down kingdom.

Jesus told us as much.) But that doesn't mean that someone who needs a little more of something to maintain peace of mind is inferior.

But they do need to make sure that their weakness leads to humility (the goal of life with God) and not arrogance.

One of the greatest challenges to life together across social divisions is always different assumptions about what people need. Someone who's spent twenty years in prison may need his own room. The son of a millionaire who's left everything to follow Jesus may need to sleep on a mat on the floor. The wisdom of the *Rule* is that we don't all have to be the same. What we all need, more than anything, is to learn to trust God and the community God has given us to supply all our needs. The first step is to thank God for what we have and to refuse to give in to complaining about other things that we might wish to have.

Kitchen Rotation

Sisters and brothers should serve one another. This is why there's no excused absence from kitchen duty unless someone is sick or busy serving the community in another capacity, for service that grows our love for one another is the goal. Anyone who needs help should have it so they can serve without frustration. As a matter of fact, everyone should have some help as the size of the community and its circumstances allow (better to work together than alone). If it's a large community, the business manager should be excused from kitchen duty, along with those we have already mentioned who are serving the community in other capacities. But let everyone else serve one another in love.

On Saturday the member who is completing her rotation will do the kitchen laundry. She should wash the hand towels that hang by the sink where members wash their hands. Along with the member who is beginning his kitchen duty, she should ritually wash all the members' hands. All the pots and pans and dishes should be washed and returned in good order to the business manager, who will re-issue them to the member starting her kitchen duty. This way, the manager can keep up with who has been given what.

An hour before mealtime, the members on kitchen duty should have a snack so they can serve the others at mealtime without a grumbling stomach or the temptation to complain. On fast days, they should wait and break the fast with everyone else.

On Sunday, just after Morning Prayer, those who are starting kitchen duty as well as those who are finishing their rotation should bow their heads in prayer and ask everyone for their prayers. The server who is completing her week should say: *Blessed are you, Lord God, who have helped me and comforted me* (Psalm 86:17b). After she says this three times, she receives a blessing. Then the one who is beginning her service says: *God, come to my assistance; Lord, make haste to help me* (Psalm 70:1b). And everyone repeats this verse together three times. When she has received a blessing, her kitchen duty begins.

CHAPTER 36
Care of the Sick

Before anything else, the community must be sure to care for its sick members, so that they may be truly served as Christ, for he said: *I was sick and you visited me* (Matthew 25:36), and: *Whatever you did for one of the least of my sisters and brothers, you did for me* (Matthew 25:40). The sick members should also remember that their sisters and brothers serve them to honor God, not to answer their every whim. They ought to take care not to weigh down with excessive demands those who care for them. Still, we must always bear patiently with the sick because serving them leads to a greater reward. For this reason, leadership should be careful that the sick are never overlooked.

A separate room should be set aside for the sick, and they should be nursed by a member who is God-fearing, attentive, and empathetic. The sick should have baths whenever it's good for their health (those who are well don't need to wash as often). To help them regain strength, the sick should be given meat. When they are well again, they can resume the normal vegetarian diet of the community.

Leadership should be especially careful that the business manager and the appointed nurses do not neglect the sick, for the shortcomings of any member in the community are their responsibility.

The Old and the Young

Even though it should come naturally for any human being to take care of the old and the young, the *Rule* should also speak up for them. Given that our bodies are weaker when we're old and need more when we're growing, seniors and youth shouldn't follow the *Rule*'s strict regulations about eating, but should be welcomed kindly to eat before everyone else.

CHAPTER 38
Reading Rotation

Public reading should always accompany the community's common meals. The reader should not be chosen haphazardly each day, but should serve in this way for a whole week at a time, beginning on Sunday. After the community's celebration of the Lord's Supper, the incoming reader should ask everyone to pray that God would protect him from thinking too highly of himself. Let him lead everyone else in praying: *Lord, open my lips, and my mouth shall proclaim your praise* (Psalm 51:15), and let everyone say it together three times. When the reader has received a blessing, he will begin his week of reading.

During meals, there should be complete silence. No talking or whispering, even—only the reader's voice should be heard. Community members should serve one another at the table, making sure everyone's needs are met without anyone having to ask for anything. If someone does need to make a request, she should signal to another member rather than speaking. No one should interrupt the reading to ask a question, *lest occasion be given to the devil* (Ephesians 4:27). The amma or abba, however, may want to offer a few words of instruction.

The reader should always have a little diluted wine before she begins reading so her mouth doesn't get dry and so she doesn't become faint. She can eat after the meal is over, along with the members who are on kitchen duty. Members should be called on to read and sing not according to their seniority in the community, but according to their ability to bless the community with their gifts.

CHAPTER 39
How Much Food to Eat

For the community's common meal each day, we believe it's enough to offer two options for the main course. That way, if someone isn't able to eat one kind of food (whether it's because they can't or because they won't), they can eat the other. But two dishes are enough for everyone to choose from. If there's fresh fruit or a salad from the garden, that can be added on the side. A nice big loaf of bread should be enough for the whole day, whether it's all eaten at one meal or spread out through the day. If the loaf is spread out through the day, it's the business manager's responsibility to set aside the extra bread for supper.

If the community is doing more manual labor than usual, the leadership may decide to give some extra food. But the leaders should be careful not to give too much—and to make sure it's not too rich—so that no one's stomach is upset by a sudden flood of sugar or oil. Nothing is as inconsistent with the Christian life as overindulgence. Our Lord says: *Take care that your hearts are not weighed down with overindulgence* (Luke 21:34a).

Kids don't need as much food as adults. In everything, frugality is the rule. Except for the sick who are very weak, the community should eat low on the food chain (no meat from large animals, just fish and chicken).

CHAPTER 40
How Much to Drink

*E*veryone has their own gift from God, one this and another that (1 Corinthians 7:7b). So we have to be careful when prescribing how much others should eat or drink (best to err on the side of liberality). Still, if we allow exceptions for the sick, we think it's fair to say that a half a bottle of wine each day is enough for each member of the community. If God gives some the strength to abstain from alcohol entirely, they know their reward.

The community's leadership may increase the daily allotment if local conditions, summer heat, or hard work require it. But they should always be careful to avoid drunkenness. We read in the Desert Fathers that monastics ought not drink wine at all, but since people today don't think this is possible, let's at least agree to drink moderately and not overdo it, *for wine makes even wise men go astray* (Sirach 19:2a).

If local circumstances require less drink—or even none at all—those who live there should bless God and not complain. Above all else, we repeat: root out the weed of complaint.

CHAPTER 41
When to Eat Together

From Easter to Pentecost, the community eats its main meal at noon and has supper in the evening. Beginning with Pentecost and continuing through the summer, everyone fasts until midafternoon on Wednesday and Friday, unless they are working in the fields or the heat is oppressive.

On other days, they eat their main meal at noon. Leadership may decide that it makes sense to eat at noon every day if most people need to be in the fields or if the heat is extreme. Leadership's job is always to set a reasonable schedule so that souls may be saved and members may go about their work without complaining.

In the fall, when the weather cools down, the community can take its main meal midafternoon. Then, during Lent, they can eat in the evening. But Evening Prayer should be scheduled so that there's still time to eat afterward in the daylight. Let nature's rhythm set the schedule: always make sure that the day's tasks can be done before the sun goes down.

EATING TO THE GLORY OF GOD

If we had to boil the *Rule* down to its basic elements, it would be fair to say they are two: how to pray and how to eat. The ladder of humility that aims to hold together the body and the spirit finds its communal expression in these shared practices. The life of the Spirit is cultivated in common prayer, just as our bodies are bound together as a single body in common meals.

In our own day, eating together may be the more countercultural practice. That people would pray together—or at least pray the same prayers in different places—is not nearly as strange a notion as the idea that people would order their lives such that they share a meal together each day. Even nuclear families find it difficult to get everyone at the same table for dinner. How, then, can a rule ask so much of people who want to journey together toward God?

Benedict knows that the table is the one place where we are all needy. So it is the place where everyone can serve. What's more, as we attend to one another's bodily needs day by day, we learn what it means to truly belong to one another. It is no accident that instructions about care for the sick come in the midst of these instructions on how to eat. The essence of community is knowing that we have the opportunity to serve Christ in a sister or brother in need—seeing that need depends on knowing one another in the mundane details of daily life. Only mouths that eat together can pray together as Christ's body.

CHAPTER 42
Silence

Always try to find space for silence, but especially at night. This should be written into the schedule: when there are two meals, everyone will sit together after supper and listen to a spiritual classic like Cassian's *Conferences* or a saint's biography—something that will benefit everyone, though it shouldn't be too hard or complicated, since it's easy for some monastics to get confused at the end of the day. Save the hard reading for another time.

At any rate, this evening reading should happen between Evening Prayer and Compline whether there's supper or not. Four or five pages should be read, as time permits. This will give everyone time to gather after finishing their assigned tasks for the day. Once everyone is together, they should pray Compline; and when they are finished, they should depart in silence. If anyone breaks this rule of silence, it should be taken very seriously (unless guests require attention or leadership needs to give special instruction; but even necessary conversation should be kept to an absolute minimum).

CHAPTER 43
Consequences for Being Late

When the bell rings for prayer, sisters and brothers should immediately leave what they're doing and hurry to the chapel (though there's no need to run or act silly). Nothing is more important than singing the eternal song that's sung around God's throne.

If anyone comes in after the *Gloria* following Psalm 95 at Vigils (that should always be said slowly, to allow time for everyone to arrive), he should not take his normal place in the choir. (Normally, members sit at prayer according to their rank—that is, their seniority in the community.) The member who's late should take the lowest place and stay there until he's had a chance to apologize to the whole community at the end of prayer. The point of this is to help the person wake up the next time. That's why, however late, no member should be turned away from prayer. If they were, they might be tempted to just go back to bed or—even worse—to stand outside chatting with someone else and thus *giving occasion to the Evil One* (Ephesians 4:27). The late brother should come inside so that all is not lost; this way, they can repent and be quicker to get up the next morning.

But if anyone arrives after grace is said and everyone has taken his seat—and if this happens because of the individual's own negligence or fault—then he should be warned the first two times (eating together is our serious business). If he still doesn't change his ways, he ought not be allowed to eat with the others, but should eat his meal alone. His allotment of wine should be taken away until he apologizes to the community and recommits to common meals. Anyone who leaves the meal early should be dealt with in the same way.

No one eats or drinks before or after the time that's set for everyone to eat together. What's more, if anyone is offered something by those in charge of the kitchen and decides not to take it, he cannot go back and ask for it later. He shouldn't be given anything until he goes back and apologizes for not taking what was offered to him.

CHAPTER 44

Reconciliation for One Who's Been Cut Off

Anyone who's been cut off from common prayer and the common table for his stubborn refusal to repent should bow down in silence at the door of the chapel when an office of prayer is ending. If he really wants to be reconciled, he should lay there at the feet of his fellow community members as they come out and not move a muscle until the leadership comes to him. If the leaders think he's ready, they should invite him to, beginning with them, bow before each member of the community and ask for their prayers. Only then should he be welcomed back into the community and assigned a new rank. He shouldn't presume to take up his former responsibilities without instructions from leadership. What's more, at every gathering for prayer, he should continue to bow down until the leadership specifically instructs him to resume a normal posture.

Those who are cut off from the table for less serious faults are to bow down at prayer only as long as the leadership instructs them to do so (the leaders will use their discretion; the amount of time may vary, depending on the offense). At any rate, the brother should maintain this public sign of humility and repentance until someone comes from leadership to bless them and says, "Enough."

CHAPTER 45
Mistakes at Prayer

I f anyone makes a mistake in a psalm; a call and response; a refrain or reading—starting too soon or stumbling over her words— she should apologize to the community. If she doesn't take this opportunity to humble herself, she should be confronted by leadership for failing to correct through humility the error that arose through negligence.

Children must be disciplined for faults at prayer so that they know from an early age that prayer is the community's serious business.

CHAPTER 46
Mistakes in Other Parts of Life

If someone makes a mistake while doing his work—in the kitchen or the storage closet, in the bakery or the garden or anywhere else—if he breaks something or loses something or messes up his work in some other way, he should immediately come before the whole community of his own accord and apologize. This should give no opportunity for shame to slip in. Make sure the person who made the mistake brings the report, and that the report doesn't get back to the community through someone else.

If the cause of a mistake is some distraction rooted in sinful thoughts, then let the person confess it privately to his spiritual director, who will know how to heal the wound without dragging it out before the whole community.

CHAPTER 47
Announcing the Hours for Prayer

L eaders should always make sure everyone knows the hours for prayer, whether by ringing the bell themselves or delegating the responsibility to someone who'll take it seriously.

Only members who are asked should lead the psalms and refrains. No one should presume to read or sing if she doesn't have that gift; the eternal song of God should be sung with humility and reverence, in all earnestness. It's not a time to mess around or show off. This is our serious business.

CHAPTER 48

Manual Labor

An idle mind is the devil's workshop. So everyone should be assigned work to do each day, in addition to the time for prayerful reading.

We believe the schedule can be set up something like this: from Easter until the beginning of fall, members go to work in the morning, from after *Prime* until about 10 AM. Then they should spend a couple of hours reading before midday prayer and lunch. After that, they should retire to their rooms for a siesta or quiet reading. They should say their afternoon prayers (*None*) at about 2:30, then go back to work until Evening Prayer.

No one should be disappointed if he has to work more because of local conditions or because the community lacks funds. If monastics live by the work of their hands, as the apostles and the Desert Mothers and Fathers did, then they are real monastics. But everything should be done in moderation, taking care not to exhaust the weak.

Through fall and winter, up until the beginning of Lent, members should do their reading in the morning, before work. After prayer at 9 AM, they should go to work until 3 PM. When the bell rings for afternoon prayers, their work is done for the day. After they eat their meal, they should devote themselves to reading, especially the Psalms.

During Lent, they should be free to read until 9 AM, after which they'll work until 4 PM. During Lent everyone is assigned a book from the library, and they should spend their free time reading it. These books are passed out at the beginning of Lent.

A couple of elders should make the rounds while members are reading to make sure no one is nodding off or getting into idle conversation with a neighbor. This is doubly dangerous because it not only distracts the members involved, but also those around them. These elders should warn anyone they find wasting the time, not only once, but twice. But if someone will not listen to them, he should be disciplined according to the *Rule* as a warning to everyone else.

On Sunday, which is a Sabbath from work, everyone should spend the day reading, unless they've been assigned to some necessary task. If anyone is unwilling or unable to use his time for study, he should be given something to do, so as not to be idle.

Those who are sick or weak should be given light work that affirms their ability to contribute but doesn't overwhelm them. Leadership is responsible for taking their infirmities into account when assigning tasks.

CHAPTER 49
Keeping Lent

The monastic life is a continuous Lent of fasting toward God's kingdom. But since there aren't many of us who are strong enough to run a marathon every day, we encourage the whole community to set aside the season of Lent as a time to refocus on our goal and strip away anything that is slowing us down in our pursuit. The best way to do this is to be diligent about unlearning bad habits and to devote ourselves to prayer with tears—to reading, to soul-searching confession, and to self-denial.

So during these days, we will add to our normal rhythms some extra fasting and time for private prayer so that each of us will have something beyond our usual sacrifice to offer to God *with the joy of the Holy Spirit* (1 Thessalonians 1:6c). Each person should choose a fast from some food or drink, or from sleep, or from needless talking, or from idle jokes. Having cast aside these things, each person should rush on toward holy Easter with joy and a renewed longing for the resurrection life.

Everyone should let leadership know ahead of time the fast that she has chosen for Lent, since it should be done with their prayers and approval. If anyone undertakes a fast without permission, she is liable to be tempted to pride, that will get her more off track than she was to start with. This is why everything should be done with leadership's approval.

CHAPTER 50

Members Who Are Away from the Community

If someone's work takes him so far away that he cannot return to the chapel for common prayer, he should pray the office where he is, and kneel out of reverence for God. As with all things, it's up to leadership to decide if this exception from common prayer is necessary.

The same goes for members who are traveling away from the community: they should keep the offices as best they can, not neglecting their measure of service.

CHAPTER 51

Those Who Make a Short Trip

If someone goes out for an errand and expects to return to the community the same day, he ought not eat outside, even if someone invites him to, unless he has permission from leadership. This is an important rule. If it's not followed, the guilty member should face the *Rule's* strongest discipline.

CHAPTER 52
The Chapel

The chapel should be a sacred space for prayer. Nothing else should be done or stored there.

After singing the eternal song, everyone should leave the space in complete silence and with reverence for God, so that someone who wants to stay and pray quietly may do so without interruption.

Anytime someone wants to pray privately, the chapel should be available to her.

No one should be loud in the space, but everyone should pray with tears and earnest devotion. If anyone is disruptive, she ought not be allowed to remain in the chapel. Don't let one person disturb everyone else's prayer.

CHAPTER 53
Welcoming Guests

Anyone who knocks at the door of the community should be welcomed as Christ, for he himself will say: *I was a stranger and you welcomed me* (Matthew 25:35c). We ought to honor the image of God in everyone, *especially those who share our faith* (Galatians 6:10c), and in pilgrims.

Once a guest's arrival has been announced, everyone should come out to greet her warmly. First, they should pray together and be united in peace; prayer should always precede a warm embrace because love is easily twisted and misunderstood.

Humility should always be demonstrated toward a guest upon their arrival and departure. With bowed heads—or even on their knees—community members should adore Christ in the guests they welcome. After guests have been greeted and invited to pray, an appointed host should sit with them. The *Rule* should be read to them so they can understand the community's life together, after which they should be served a meal. The host may break a normal fast for the sake of guests, but everyone else should keep theirs. The host should wash the guests' hands herself, and the whole community should come together to wash their feet. When the foot washing is done, they say together: *God, we have received your mercy within your temple* (Psalm 48:9).

Be especially careful and eager to welcome poor people and pilgrims, because Christ is received more particularly in them. Our natural response to the rich guarantees that they'll be taken care of.

A separate dining area should be set aside for the host and guests, so that guests—a monastic community will always have them—won't disturb the normal rhythm of life. Each year, two members who can do the job well should be assigned to manage this dining room for guests. If they need it, additional help should be provided so they can do their job without temptation to complain. If, however, there aren't guests to be served at any time, they should serve wherever there's another job that needs to be done. Note: this applies not only to them, but also to everyone. If someone needs help, the community helps them; if someone is free, she works wherever she's needed.

Another member should be put in charge of hospitality rooms for guests. He should make sure the accommodations are in good order. Make sure he's a God-fearing brother who will manage resources wisely.

Other members shouldn't strike up conversation with guests unless they're asked to. If they meet a guest on the grounds, they should greet them humbly. They should ask for a blessing and continue on their way, explaining that they're not allowed to have side conversations.

WALLS WITH AN OPEN GATE

No community exists without boundaries. To give yourself to particular people in a particular place is to make public one's circle of belonging. But like any circle, this one demarcates a line between those who are "inside" and those who are not.

This is a danger inherent to any human community. Most people experience relationships that change (or are lost) when friends give themselves to someone new in marriage. The same thing can happen when someone joins a new group of friends, takes a new job, or has kids. No one has an unlimited capacity for relationship with others. To truly belong to a people is to be something of a stranger to everyone else.

Still, these divisions between the various spheres of our lives can be more and less healthy. An ethnic community that sticks together in exile, sharing food and language that would otherwise be lost, can be a great gift to the individuals within it, as well as the place where it exists. But at the same time, an ethnic community that cares for its own can harbor animosity or even hatred for another group. Healthy community requires both stability and generosity—a sense of human limits combined with a broad appreciation of shared humanity.

These chapters on travel and hospitality demonstrate Benedict's wisdom with regard to boundaries. Every member's primary allegiance must be to God in the community.

Because people are so easily distracted, Benedict guards the boundaries closely: members are to keep the community's rhythm, even when they're away. They're to fast as long as a full day and then hurry home and eat with the family. They're not to talk to anyone from outside the community without permission. These boundaries are so firm as to seem extreme to us.

But, at the same time, Benedict recognizes the danger of a community becoming a fortress against the "enemy at the gates." Thus, as a rule, the gate must be always open. A member should always be ready to play host to guests—and every guest must be welcomed as if he was Jesus himself. A community that is centered around the worship of God, then, is always poised to greet the God who shows up at the edges, looking every bit like a beggar and just wanting a place to stay. The integrity of this peculiar people depends not on self-defense, but on hospitality. Because it is God who holds this body together, not strength of effort or will.

CHAPTER 54
Letters or Gifts for Members

Members are not allowed to exchange letters or gifts with their parents or anyone else without permission from the community's leadership. They should not presume to receive a package even from their own family without first telling leadership. The leaders should decide who in the community most needs the gift, and the member for whom it was sent should not worry about it, *lest occasion be given to the Evil One* (Ephesians 4:27, 1 Timothy 5:14b). If anyone decides to act otherwise, he will be subject to the discipline of the *Rule*.

CHAPTER 55
Clothes and Shoes for Members

What members wear will vary according to the local climate and conditions. A lot is left to the discretion of those in leadership. We believe that simple pants, shirt, and a pullover will be enough in temperate climates. In colder climates a winter coat is needed—where it's hotter, a T-shirt. Everyone should have a pair of overalls for work. And everyone needs shoes—both a sturdy pair for work and travel and house shoes to wear at home.

No one should complain about the color of the clothes assigned to them or the quality of the fabric. The community should simply use whatever is available locally and at a reasonable cost. Those in leadership should make sure that the clothes fit the members, paying special attention not to assign clothes that are too small.

Whenever new clothes are distributed, the old should be donated to a clothes closet or thrift store. So that everyone always has clothes to wear while dirty ones are being laundered, members should be given two of everything. Anything more than that is unnecessary. Any time a new article of clothing is received, the old one should be given away.

If members are going on a trip and will need more than their single extra set of clothes, they should ask for extras from the supply closet. When they return home, they should wash what they borrowed and return it to its place. They can also check out a nicer coat to wear when they are out on community business, but they should return it when they get back.

For bedding, each person needs a mattress, sheets, a pillow, and a blanket.

Bedrooms should be inspected occasionally to make sure no one is hoarding something as his own private property. This is a serious offense that must be addressed immediately. The job of a community's leaders is to provide everything an individual needs so that the bad habit of calling something *my own* can be rooted out of everyone's soul. So, let each person be issued pants, shirt, coat, and shoes, a belt, pen, notebook, towel, and toiletry bag. This way everyone can be assured that his needs will be met and that he need not fend for himself.

But those in leadership should also always remember the words from Acts: *Distribution was made to each according to their needs* (Acts 4:35b). So the leadership should always consider the weakness of the needy, not the potential for jealousy that still lingers in someone else's heart. In every consideration, they should recall their responsibility before almighty God.

CHAPTER 56
The Leaders' Table

The leaders have a separate table where they serve as hosts to guests and travelers. Whenever there are no guests, they may invite any of the members they choose to come and eat with them. But for the sake of maintaining order, a couple of elders should always remain at the tables with other members.

Artists in the Community

If there are artists in the community, they should practice their craft humbly, with permission from those in leadership. If someone is tempted by pride because of his great skill, or if he thinks too highly of his contribution to the community, he should be instructed to stop practicing his craft. He shouldn't be given permission to resume until he shows signs of real humility. After all, no art is more important than climbing the ladder of humility.

When the works of artists in the community are sold, those members responsible for the sale must be honest in their dealings. They should always remember Ananias and Sapphira (Acts 5:1–11), lest they be tempted to fraud and suffer spiritual death.

Greed must not play any part in the setting of prices. The community should always be able to offer products below market value, *so that in all things God may be glorified* (1 Peter 4:11c).

CHAPTER 58

Membership in the Community

D on't make it easy to join the community, but as John says: *Test the spirits to see if they are from God* (1 John 4:1b). So if someone comes to join, let him knock at the door for four or five days. If he's persistent and not deterred, then invite him in as a guest for a few days. After that, he should join the novices, who study, eat, and sleep together.

An elder who's known for her skill in evangelism should be assigned to watch over the novices. Here's what she should watch for: people who are genuinely seeking after God; who are eager to sing the eternal song; who listen well; and who don't mind dealing with difficult tasks and people. She should make this clear to every novice: the road that leads to God is uphill and strewn with roadblocks. This life is not for the spiritual gadabouts.

If the novice is determined to stick with the community, then after two months this *Rule* should be read to him cover to cover. And he should be told, "This is the law under which you're choosing to serve. If you can keep it, join us. If not, feel free to leave." If he stands his ground, then he should go back to the novitiate for six months. Then, the *Rule* should be read to him again to make sure he knows what he's getting himself into. If he stands firm again, then test him for another four months (now he's been in the novitiate a full year). If after taking time to reflect he promises to keep every commandment and to listen well, then welcome him into the community. But make sure he understands that, according to the *Rule*, he's no longer free to leave or to get out from under the obligations of the *Rule*. Up until now, he's been a practicing member of the community, free to stay or go. But from this point on, he's committed for life.

When he is to be received as a member, he stands before the whole community in the chapel and promises to stay, to live the monastic way, and to listen. All of this happens before God and the community to impress upon the novice that he is taking a solemn vow. He makes his promise in writing, there in front of everyone. If he is illiterate, he asks someone else to write for him. But he signs it himself, and lays it on the altar with his own hand. After he has put it there, he says: *Receive me, Lord, as you have promised, and I shall live; do not disappoint me in my hope* (Psalm 119:116). The whole community joins him, and the members repeat the verse three times, ending with a *Gloria*. Then the novice bows down before each member and asks for his prayers. From that very day, he is a community member.

If he has any possessions, he should either give them to the poor before he comes or donate them to the community, along with his very self. Right there in the chapel he should take off everything that belonged to him before and receive his allotment of clothes from the community. What he takes off should be kept in a closet so that, in the event that he ever gives into the enemy's suggestion and leaves, he can be sent out in those clothes and not in the uniform of the community. The document that he laid on the altar before everyone should be filed away in the community's records.

CHAPTER 59
On Children Offered to God in the Community

If an important family decides to offer a child to God in the community, the parents write out the document described above. When the time comes for the donation of goods, the family members wrap the document and the child's hand both in the altar cloth. This is how they make their offering.

As for property, the parents either promise that they will never themselves nor through someone else try to give their child anything, or, if they can't bear to do this, they make a donation to the community. But this promise, in writing, should make it clear to their child that she should never expect to be shown favor because of noble birth. God forbid that the thought should cross anyone's mind, but we have seen it happen.

Poor people can do the very same, but those who have nothing simply write the document and, in the presence of witnesses, offer their child to the Lord.

CHAPTER 60
On Clergy Joining the Community

I f ordained clergy want to join the community, don't agree to their
joining too quickly. If they persist, make it clear that they will have
to have to follow the *Rule* like everyone else—no exceptions. For it's
written: *Friend, what have you come for?* (Matthew 26:50a).

Still, if clergy join, they should be allowed to offer blessings and
celebrate communion, provided that those in leadership ask them to.
Otherwise, they should follow the *Rule* like everyone else, not making exceptions for themselves. If they're to be an example in any way,
it should be in humility. Clergy don't get to jump rank when it's time
for a new appointment to leadership. They're just like everyone else;
their rank is based on when they arrived, not on their status as clergy.

People who've served the church at lower levels—as deacons or
housekeepers—can get some credit for their experience. (Humble
service, after all, is the only way to climb the ladder in this rule.) If
they come to join the community, they should be ranked somewhere
in the middle of the members, but only if they promise to follow the
Rule and stay.

CHAPTER 61
Visitors from Other Communities

A member of a sister community may want to come and stay as a guest. As long as she is content with things as she finds them and doesn't make too many demands, she should be welcomed to stay as long as she wants. In humility and love, she may indeed point out something that could be done better or that has been overlooked. The community's leadership should listen carefully to these observations, for it may be that the Lord sent this sister for the very purpose of helping them see something they could not see on their own.

If the guest wants to commit herself and promises to stay, she shouldn't be turned away, especially since there will have been time to judge her character while she was a guest. But if she has been a difficult guest, by all means don't welcome her in as a member! Instead, she should be asked to leave as politely as possible, lest her attitude infect others in the community.

If she hasn't demonstrated that she's a difficult person, then welcome her as a member if she asks to become one. She should even be encouraged to stay so that others can learn from her good example. After all, we serve the same Lord and work for the same cause wherever we may be in God's good world.

Those in leadership may choose to place such a person in a somewhat higher place in the community, if they can see that she deserves it. As a matter of fact, they have the freedom to change anyone's rank, so long as their character warrants it (and not just their social class or ecclesial position).

But note: a community should never receive a member from a sister community unless that community's leadership approves and sends a letter of recommendation. For we know the Scripture that says: *Never do to another what you do not want done to yourself* (Tobit 4:16).

CHAPTER 62

The Community's Clergy

Any community that asks to have one of its members ordained should offer for ordination someone who is worthy to serve as a representative of Christ. The candidate should be careful to guard herself against pride and conceit. Obedience to the community is key, along with the recognition that this office will make it all the more important to follow the *Rule* closely. Clergy need the ladder of humility more than anyone if they are to continue climbing toward God.

Ordained clergy should always be careful to not pull rank and assume privilege because of their status. They are only set apart for their service at the altar. If the community chooses to grant them a higher rank, it should be for the holiness of their lives, not the importance of their job. Just as with other roles in the community, if the job becomes a source of pride, it should be taken away. Someone who clings to his office at the expense of his soul is a rebel, not a priest.

If clergy will not listen to the warnings of the community, a church official may be called in to help. If that does not cause them to repent, the rebellious clergy should be asked to leave the community—but only as a last resort, if they're so arrogant they won't listen at all.

CHAPTER 63
Rank in the Community

Community members are assigned rank based on when they arrive, how they live, and what the leadership decides. Leaders should be careful not to stir up trouble by making unjust assignments. Their power should not be used arbitrarily, but with a constant awareness that they must give an account to God for every decision and action.

Whenever the community takes communion or gathers in the chapel for prayer, they do so according to the rank assigned to them. Age should never automatically determine rank. After all, Samuel and Daniel were still boys when they judged their elders (1 Samuel 3; Daniel 13:44–62). So unless leadership has decided to promote or demote someone for one of the reasons mentioned above, everyone should keep the rank assigned to him when he joined the community. For example, someone who came to the community in its second year has to recognize that he is a junior to someone who was there at the beginning, regardless of his age or education level. Children, however, should always be considered juniors to all the adults.

Newer members should respect their elders, and those who've been around longer should love the newcomers. When they speak to one another, they shouldn't call each other by name, like strangers do, but with terms of endearment, as a family would. Elders should call their juniors "brother" or "sister," while younger members should call their elders "mama" or "papa." Leaders in the community should be called by a special name, because they represent Christ to the community. Just as the disciples called Jesus "Master," members of the community should call those in leadership "mother" or "father," not because they deserve such a title, but because they represent Christ. For their own sake, though, leaders should always reflect on what they are called, considering whether they are worthy of such an honor.

Whenever members meet, the junior member should ask her elder for a blessing. She should always offer her seat to someone of higher rank and shouldn't presume to sit down unless her elder invites her to. In this way, every member should strive to do what the Scriptures say: *They should each try to be the first to show respect to the other* (Romans 12:10b).

In the chapel or at the dinner table, children should be watched over by the adult members as a group, according to their ages. Elsewhere, and at other times, the community should take care to supervise and discipline them as needed until they are old enough to be responsible for themselves.

The Election of Leaders

When electing leaders, the guiding principle should always be consensus. Members submit willingly to the leadership of those whom they elect. A good life and wisdom are what everyone should look for in potential leaders, even if the person who possessed these things holds the lowest rank.

God forbid that a whole community would conspire together to elect someone who's willing to overlook bad habits and endorse evil actions. But if this happens, then the church should intervene—whether it's local church leadership or representatives of sister communities or just other Christians in the area. Someone must step in so that the whole community will not be ruined. Whoever does this can be sure that, as long as he does it with pure motives and genuine concern, he will receive a reward from the Lord. To not intervene when something like this happens is itself a sin.

Once in their office, community leaders should always keep in mind the gravity of their task and remember to whom they will have *to give an account of their stewardship* (cf. Luke 16:2). Their aim is always the good of the members, not their own well-being. So they should be careful students of Scripture, building up a storehouse of knowledge out of which they can bring *some things old and some things new* (Matthew 13:52c). They should be in control of their own desires and merciful with others, always *letting mercy triumph over judgment* (James 2:13b) so that they too may receive mercy. They must hate the things that trip members up, but love the members all the same time. When they have to apply the discipline of the *Rule*, leaders should be careful and avoid extremes. If you scrub a stain too hard, you can tear right through the piece of clothing. So leaders should always consider their judgments carefully and remember *not to crush the bruised reed* (Isaiah 42:3a). They shouldn't allow people to flounder in bad habits, but instead should prune them carefully, like a gardener who knows what's best for each plant. Leaders should strive to be loved rather than feared.

They should not be quick-tempered, anxious, extreme, obstinate, jealous, or overly suspicious. Such people can never rest. (It would be a curse to put them in charge of a community.) Leaders should, instead, demonstrate consideration in their decisions. Whether they're assigning a task that is divine or mundane, they should be careful, recalling the discretion of Jacob, who said: *If I drive my flocks too hard, they will all die in a single day* (Genesis 33:13b). This kind of discretion is the mother of virtues for leaders. Leaders must manage the community such that the strong have something to strive toward and the weak have nothing to run from.

Leaders must, above all else, follow the *Rule* themselves, so that when their job is done they will hear from the Lord what the good servant heard who gave his fellow servants grain at the appropriate time: *I tell you the truth*, he said, *he sets him over all his possessions* (Matthew 24:47).

CHAPTER 65
Assistants to Leadership

When assistants to leadership are appointed, it has too often caused contention in communities. Some assistants get a big head and start to think of themselves as "second-in-command," grabbing after power and sowing seeds of discord in the community. This has often happened in communities where the same process was used to elect both the leadership and the assistants. It's easy to see why this is a bad arrangement; from the very start, the assistants are tempted to pride. They too easily imagine that they are exempt from leadership's authority. *After all*, they say to themselves, *I was elected by the same people who chose them.*

This is an open invitation to envy, infighting, bad-mouthing, competition, and divisions. When leaders and assistants don't work together, their own souls are endangered while at the same time the community members are pressured to take sides and thereby ruin themselves. The responsibility for such a mess rests with those who set up a terrible process to start with.

Here is a better way: once leadership has been elected, let them make all appointments in the community. If possible, as we said above, the whole community should be managed by small group leaders. But all of these people should be appointed to their tasks by the elected leadership. This is the best way to keep from tempting anyone to pride.

If a community is large enough that the leadership needs assistants, let them be appointed also, with advice from God-fearing members. The assistants should do what they're asked to do with respect and not go their own way when they think they know better than leadership what should be done in a given circumstance. As with all positions of authority in the community, the more power someone has, the more careful she should be to follow the *Rule* faithfully.

If assistants are found to have serious faults, or become conceited and give into pride, or refuse to follow the *Rule*, they should be warned as many as four times. But if they don't change their ways, they must be disciplined according to the *Rule*. If they still will not change, they should be removed from their office and replaced by someone who's worthy of the position. If after all of this an assistant cannot return to being a peaceful and obedient member of the community, he should be asked to leave the community.

As always, though, the leaders should recall that they have to give an account to God for every decision, lest the fire of jealousy or rivalry flare up and consume their soul.

SEEDS OF DEMOCRACY

Historians of Western civilization have noted how the seeds of democracy were planted by communities that lived Benedict's *Rule* in the midst of an extremely hierarchical society with little opportunity for social mobility. During the Dark Ages, communities that welcomed rich and poor alike, assigning rank based on when a member arrived, presented a radical counterculture. Anyone who paid attention could see that another world was possible.

But from our own perspective, on this side of the twentieth century's liberation movements, Benedict's concern for rank and leadership can seem itself hierarchical. Many people are drawn to intentional forms of community because of the sense of marginalization they experience in mainstream society. If the ladder that most people are trying to climb seems so oppressive, it can seem like it'd be better to do away with ladders all together. Why not have a community that's committed to seeing everyone as equals?

Benedict seems to know two things from experience: one is that when something is everyone's responsibility, it's no one's responsibility. Yes, power goes with responsibility, and power can be abused. But the alternative to bad leadership isn't no leadership. Benedict knows the alternative is good leadership. And because he knows this, he knows a second truth that's essential to healthy community: people are glad to listen to leaders whose example and wisdom they've had a chance to affirm. Democracy is about as close as human society has come to this on a large scale. But community is a great place to experiment with the kind of consensus building that makes true democracy sustainable.

CHAPTER 66
The Community's Doorkeeper

By the door of the community, place a sensible older member who has basic secretarial skills and is glad to sit and welcome people. This member will need a room close to the entrance so that visitors will always find him there to answer them. As soon as anyone comes knocking or asking for help, he should say, "Praise the Lord," or, "Blessings," as he answers the door promptly with all the warmth of God's love. If he needs help with this job, the doorkeeper should be assigned a younger member as an assistant.

The community should be set up to provide for its own needs as much as possible, keeping a garden and making what the members can for themselves. This cuts down on the members' need to be away, which isn't good for their souls.

Read this *Rule* often to the community. It's important, and we don't want anyone to say they forgot it.

◇ CHAPTER 67 ◇
Members Traveling Away from the Community

When members are sent on a trip away from the community, they should ask everyone for her prayers. Any members who are absent should be remembered at the closing prayer each time the community gathers for common prayer. When they return, they should bow down before everyone in the chapel, asking for their prayers. There are so many things that can distract a monastic or disturb her thoughts when she's on the road.

No one who's been away should go on and on about the things she heard and saw while away from the community. This can cause all kinds of trouble in a community. If anyone does go on and on, she should be disciplined according to the *Rule*. Likewise, anyone who tries to leave, or go anywhere, or do anything at all—even if it seems quite small—without direction from leadership, should be disciplined according to the *Rule*.

CHAPTER 68

Requests That Seem Unreasonable

If members are asked to do something they think they cannot do, they should listen carefully to the order and receive it with humility. If after they have tried to do it they still don't think it is possible, they should go back to the leadership at an appropriate time and explain why the task is too hard for them. They ought not be proud or angry; they are simply reporting the facts as they see them. If the leadership does not see a need to reassign the task, then the one who's received it must recognize that continuing to do the same task is best for him. Trusting in God's help, he must listen and obey in love.

CHAPTER 69

On Not Defending Fellow Members

Every member should be careful not to defend a brother or sister in the community or to try and stand up for them, no matter how close their relationship. This is important; it can tear a community apart. Anyone who breaks this rule must be confronted immediately.

CHAPTER 70
On Not Attacking Fellow Members

While members must not defend one another, they cannot attack or lash out at one another either. This, too, is presumption. No one is to judge another in any way or attempt to discipline him unless he receives specific instructions from leadership. *Those who sin should be reprimanded in front of everyone, so that the rest may fear* (1 Timothy 5:20). Children, however, should be supervised by everyone until they are adolescents. This should be done with moderation and common sense.

If anyone assumes power over someone else without orders—or even if someone treats kids unreasonably—he should be disciplined according to the *Rule. Never do to another what you do not want done to yourself* (Tobit 4:16).

CHAPTER 71
Listening to One Another

We should be willing to listen to everyone—not just those in leadership, but every member—for we know that we go to God by the way of obedience. Of course, it is always important to listen to leadership. But members should also be eager to listen to one another and to help where they can. Anyone who objects to this should be corrected.

If anyone in the community is corrected—or if someone even gets the feeling that someone else is angry with him—he should bow down before the person right then and there and ask forgiveness. He ought not to get up off the ground until his fellow community member has blessed him. This is how unity is maintained—through mutual submission to one another out of reverence for Christ. Anyone who will not learn and follow this way cannot remain as part of the community.

CHAPTER 72
The Right Kind of Passion

Just as there are bad passions that lead us away from God to our own destruction, so too there are good passions that set us on fire to chase after God and the life that's really life. This is the right kind of passion that monastics must foster with fervent love: *They should each try to be the first to show respect to the other* (Romans 12:10b). We're on this road together, and so we must patiently bear with one another's spiritual and physical weaknesses, giving our all to learn to listen carefully to one another. No one should look after himself, but each one should strive to serve the others in everything. To one another, members should show pure love; to God, loving reverence; to leadership, humble love. We should not want anything more than Christ, who can bring us together to the life that lasts forever.

CHAPTER 73
The Rule *Is Only a Place to Begin*

We've written this *Rule* so that communities that follow it can have a place to begin the monastic life. But for anyone who's eager to press on toward the goal, we have the teachings of all those saints who've gone before us. Listen to them if you want to find the life that's really life. Pay attention to every verse of the Old and New Testaments, for we know no truer guide for human life. We have a library of classics to consult alongside the Scriptures, beginning with *The Wisdom of the Desert Fathers and Mothers*, Cassian's *Conferences* and *Institutes*, Basil's *Rule*, and the lives of all the saints. For those who are willing to listen, these are the tools we need to break up the hard soil of our lives and sow a garden of virtues. Too often, reading the Christian classics makes us feel inadequate—even ashamed. Why don't we rush on toward real life like the saints of old? But with Christ's help, this little *Rule* can be a place to begin. Start here. Then you can climb on to the higher summits of teaching and virtue mentioned above, and under God's protection you will reach them. Amen.

FURTHER READING

In celebration of Benedict's fifteen-hundredth birthday, leaders of contemporary Benedictine communities commissioned a new English translation of the *Rule*. Indispensible for anyone who wants to be a serious student of Benedict today, it is available in two forms—a small one, like this volume, that is simply a translation of the *Rule*, and a large, six-hundred-page volume that includes historical essays, critical notes on the Latin text, and appendices about scholarly issues in the study of the *Rule*. See *RB 1980: The Rule of Saint Benedict in Latin and English with Notes*, ed. Timothy Fry, OSB (Liturgical Press, 1980).

Benedict's *Rule* is a wonderful introduction to the spiritual wisdom that Benedict himself inherited. He concludes his own work by recommending further reading in the classics of his own day. Fifteen hundred years later, there are other Christian classics to recommend, many of which were written by people who lived their lives according to the *Rule*. One great place to begin exploring the Christian classics is the Renovare resource *25 Books Every Christian Should Read* (HarperOne, 2011), that includes introductions to a wide range of classics along with excerpts from each one. The Paraclete Essentials series, of which this book is a part, offers beautiful paperback editions of good contemporary translations for about a dozen of these works. For groups that want to explore the classics together, Paraclete also offers a five-session DVD curriculum, *Discovering Christian Classics*.

In addition to this rich wisdom from church history, there are also several good contemporary writers who explore how Benedict can guide us today. Kathleen Norris is perhaps the most well-known writer among them, having written the *New York Times* bestsellers *The Cloister Walk* and *Dakota*. The popularity of her books is a testament not only to her skill as a writer, but also to her striking ability to hear the *Rule* speaking to the everyday struggles of marriage and depression, small town life and airplane travel. Norris is an oblate who has committed herself to live by the *Rule* as much as possible in her life outside the monastery. Her work has led to a significant growth in oblate ministry for Benedictine monasteries in North America. You can learn more about what it means to become an oblate by contacting the Benedictine community closest to you: http://www.osb.org/geog/searchform.asp

No monastic writer of the twentieth century was better known than Thomas Merton, whose many works on the monastic life are still in print. M. Basil Pennington, Joan Chittister, Michael Casey, Jeremy Hall, and many others have continued Benedict's tradition of writing from the monastery to the world. Chittister's *The Radical Christian Life: A Year with Saint Benedict* (Liturgical Press, 2011) would be a good follow-up read for people who want to sit with the *Rule* for an extended time and ask how it might shape their life.

NOTES AND ACKNOWLEDGMENTS

B enedict's *Rule*, like his own life, is saturated in Scripture. Like many ancient writers (and some contemporary pastors), Benedict quotes Scripture from memory, often adjusting its wording to fit the syntax of his sentence or the specific context he is addressing. This is not accidental. Benedict believes that the word of God is "alive and active—sharper than a diamond-cut razor" (Hebrews 4:12b). Scripture is not in its truest form when it rigidly adheres to the ancient manuscripts, but it is when it speaks God's truth directly to our lives. As much as possible, I have indicated in italics when Benedict is quoting or alluding to Scripture. Following him, I have not quoted any particular contemporary English translation but have rather paraphrased Benedict's own rendering.

Anyone who wants to practice the cycles of prayer Benedict lays out in chapters 8 to 20 would do well to get a copy of *Benedictine Daily Prayer: A Short Breviary*, complied and edited by Maxwell E. Johnson and the monks of Saint John's Abbey (Liturgical Press, 2005). In some two thousand pages, with six colored ribbons, this volume is a guide to the contemporary practice of Benedictine prayer. For anyone who is intimidated by seven daily offices and the page turning that requires six ribbons, there are two contemporary resources for fixed-hour prayer that are influenced by the Benedictine tradition but are much simpler. Phyllis Tickle's *The Divine Hours* is a beautiful guide for daily individual use. *Common Prayer: A Liturgy for Ordinary Radicals*, that I helped compile, is great for individuals and groups. It has a special focus on integrating prayer and action in our world.

I have Michael Cartwright to thank for gently and consistently reminding me that any "new monasticism" must be constantly looking back to its sources, paying attention to the wisdom of those who've gone before us. At his suggestion, Jon Stock, Tim Otto, and I wrote *Inhabiting the Church: Biblical Wisdom for a New Monasticism* (Cascade Books, 2006) on the three Benedictine promises of stability, obedience, and conversion. Though I wrote on conversion for that project, the time I spent with the *Rule* interested me in stability. I was amazed by all that the Benedictine tradition had to offer those of us who are trying to make sense of life and faith in a hypermobile culture. *The Wisdom of Stability* (Paraclete Press, 2010) grew out of that fascination and the many gifts that came as I followed where it led.

Living traditions are summed up in texts, but they are passed on through lives and friendship. When I read the *Rule*, I feel like I can hear Benedict speaking to me, because I spent hours listening to Abbot Timothy Kelley. It's a testimony to Benedictine hospitality that a community would lend someone of Timothy's stature to a guest like me. But Timothy and the monks of Saint John's Abbey are living proof that human beings can make progress on the ladder of humility. This paraphrase is dedicated to Timothy with gratitude for his friendship and his life.

DISCUSSION GUIDE

To Be Used in Conjunction with This Book and the Video
The Rule of Saint Benedict: An Introduction

These questions are best discussed by two or more people who are reading this book and have watched the video *The Rule of Saint Benedict: An Introduction*.

1. Why have you decided to study Benedict and his *Rule*? What do you hope monastic wisdom can offer you and your community?

2. As you read the *Rule*, where does Benedict seem sensitive to human limitations and weakness? How does he balance the radical call of discipleship with sustainable expectations?

3. Jonathan notes that the *Rule* proposed an alternative social order in the midst of the Dark Ages. How do you see the patterns and practices of the *Rule* challenging today's social norms?

4. How might the posture of a "spiritual seeker" make us "slaves to our own will"? Why is Benedict concerned about this, and what promise does the practice of stability offer?

5. Why is obedience difficult for us? How does the *Rule* safeguard against abuses of authority? Why does Benedict think learning to listen is so important to our growth in Christlikeness?

6. What does the *Rule* propose as a plan for how we can learn to be always listening to God?

7. What practices in your own life "bring you back to God"? Are there new practices you've learned from the *Rule* that you'd like to adopt? What might they look like?

8. How did Dorothy Day put the *Rule* into practice during the Great Depression? What might hospitality look like in your community?

9. What rhythms of prayer and work shape your life? Whether you're together or not, how do you share those rhythms with others?

10. Is work a gift to your spiritual life? In what ways might your work be "out of rhythm"?

11. How does the *Rule* teach us to read Scripture together? Are there spaces in your life where you might practice *lectio divina*?

12. What does it mean for humility to be "at the center" of the *Rule*? Who are the models of humility that we celebrate? How do we grow up into humility?

ABOUT PARACLETE PRESS

WHO WE ARE

Paraclete Press is a publisher of books, recordings, and DVDs on Christian spirituality. Our publishing represents a full expression of Christian belief and practice—from Catholic to Evangelical, from Protestant to Orthodox.

We are the publishing arm of the Community of Jesus, an ecumenical monastic community in the Benedictine tradition. As such, we are uniquely positioned in the marketplace without connection to a large corporation and with informal relationships to many branches and denominations of faith.

WHAT WE ARE DOING

PARACLETE PRESS BOOKS | Paraclete publishes books that show the richness and depth of what it means to be Christian. Although Benedictine spirituality is at the heart of all that we do, we publish books that reflect the Christian experience across many cultures, time periods, and houses of worship. We publish books that nourish the vibrant life of the church and its people.

We have several different series, including the best-selling Paraclete Essentials and Paraclete Giants series of classic texts in contemporary English; Voices from the Monastery—men and women monastics writing about living a spiritual life today; award-winning poetry; best-selling gift books for children on the occasions of baptism and first communion; and the Active Prayer Series that brings creativity and liveliness to any life of prayer.

MOUNT TABOR BOOKS | Paraclete's newest series, Mount Tabor Books, focuses on liturgical worship, art and art history, ecumenism, and the first millennium church, and was created in conjunction with the Mount Tabor Ecumenical Centre for Art and Spirituality in Barga, Italy.

PARACLETE RECORDINGS | From Gregorian chant to contemporary American choral works, our recordings celebrate the best of sacred choral music composed through the centuries that create a space for heaven and earth to intersect. Paraclete Recordings is the record label representing the internationally acclaimed choir Gloriæ Dei Cantores, praised for their "rapt and fathomless spiritual intensity" by *American Record Guide*; the Gloriæ Dei Cantores Schola, specializing in the study and performance of Gregorian chant; and the other instrumental artists of the Gloriæ Dei Artes Foundation.

Paraclete Press is also privileged to be the exclusive North American distributor of the recordings of the Monastic Choir of St. Peter's Abbey in Solesmes, France, long considered to be a leading authority on Gregorian chant.

PARACLETE VIDEO | Our DVDs offer spiritual help, healing, and biblical guidance for a broad range of life issues including grief and loss, marriage, forgiveness, facing death, bullying, addictions, Alzheimer's, and spiritual formation.

Learn more about us at our website:
www.paracletepress.com or phone us
toll-free at 1.800.451.5006

SCAN
TO
READ
MORE

Also available in Paraclete Essentials Deluxe Editions...

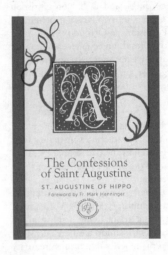

THE CONFESSIONS OF ST. AUGUSTINE
Saint Augustine

ISBN 978-1-61261-771-8
$17.99, Leatherette

The first autobiography ever written, and one of the most profound testaments of faith, ever.

REVELATIONS OF DIVINE LOVE
Julian of Norwich

ISBN 978-1-61261-770-1
$17.99, Leatherette

This translation presents Julian's work in a style and format that breaks through not only to her deepest meanings, but also to the character of the gentle woman herself.

Available at bookstores everywhere.
Paraclete Press
1-800-451-5006
www.paracletepress.com